A Wealth of Wisdom

WHAT THE PAST CAN TEACH US ABOUT PLANNING FOR THE FUTURE

NICOLAS DAVIS, CFP®, CHFC®
RICP®

BRINDLE & BAY WEALTH MANAGEMENT

Nicolas Davis/Brindle & Bay Wealth Management

5899 Preston Rd., Suite 1103

Frisco, TX 75034

https://brindleandbay.com

A Wealth of Wisdom / Nicolas Davis 2nd ed.

ISBN 9798708059680

The contents of this book are provided for informational purposes only and are not intended to serve as the basis for any financial decisions. Any tax, legal or estate planning information is general in nature. It should not be construed as legal or tax advice. Always consult an attorney or tax professional regarding the applicability of this information to your unique situation.

The content of this book should not be construed as personalized investment advice, nor should it be interpreted as an offer to buy or sell any securities mentioned. A financial advisor should be consulted before implementing any of the strategies presented.

Investing involves risk, including the potential loss of principal. No investment strategy can guarantee a profit or protect against loss in periods of declining values. Any references to protection benefits or guaranteed/lifetime income streams refer only to fixed insurance products, not securities or investment products. Insurance and annuity product guarantees are backed by the financial strength and claims-paying ability of the issuing insurance company.

We do not provide tax or legal advice. You are expressly advised to consult with a qualified attorney or tax professional to determine your legal or tax needs.

Investment advisory services offered through Brindle & Bay Financial Advisors, LLC, a Registered Investment Adviser.

Table of Content

Preface

August 13, 1955. Does that date mean anything to you?

From the beginning, 1955 was an eventful year. Television was on the rise; on January 19, Dwight D. Eisenhower became the first president to have his news conference broadcast on TV. On March 3, Elvis Presley followed up with his first television appearance. A month later, on April 12, Dr. Jonas Salk's polio vaccine was declared safe and effective. Three days after that, a slightly less healthy substance hit the market when Ray Kroc opened his first McDonald's restaurant in Des Plaines, Illinois. On June 30, *The Johnny Carson Show* debuted, and on September 30, iconic actor James Dean died in a tragic car crash.

The year was marked by social change, civil rights activism, a rising hippie movement and the looming threat of nuclear war. Many remarkable events would shift the course of American history. But for me, August 13 was the most important day in 1955. That's the day my grandparents, Leroy and Betty, were married. That year, Leroy graduated from high school and four months later he was married to Betty. They had quickly fallen in love, married, and started a family, all in a small town in Illinois.

Grandpa Leroy did everything right. To support his young family, Leroy took up bricklaying. He built a 900-square-foot ranch-style home across the street from where he had graduated high school. That very house was where he and Betty raised three children. I remember that house fondly; I spent many days there in my youth under Grandpa's tutelage. I'd often stop by after school when I attended the same school.

Leroy excelled at his trade. His reputation grew until he was known around the Midwest for his ornately bricked Catholic Churches. During his time as a bricklayer, there were no computers or design software to help him out. The best you'd get was a piece of paper. But Grandpa didn't even need that. He could design a cathedral in his head and then build it with his own hands. If you wanted fancy brickwork, you called my grandpa, Leroy.

In 1995, Leroy retired and started collecting a reasonable pension from the bricklayer's union, which was solvent at the time. Over the years he'd acquired three rental properties which supplemented his retirement income. Grandpa was only sixty when he retired, and he had enough that he could buy the family a new van every three years and take it on vacation often nearly every year. He took up woodworking to stay busy. By the time he passed away, he had not one, but two workshops stuffed to the ceiling with things he'd designed and built. Not bad for a bricklayer from Illinois, right? Like I said, he did everything right.

I had the privilege of seeing my grandpa and his hard work and determination throughout his life. He was my mentor. In fact, he helped me catch my first fish, and he taught me how to use a table scroll saw and taught me my first money lessons. I remember he'd say, "Nici (that was my childhood nickname), *never* invest in life insurance." He'd give me advice like, "Your credit is everything; the bank won't give you money unless they know you don't need it."

When Leroy earned his living, those adages may have been true. He was opinionated, but his financial creed worked. When I was sixteen, Grandpa took me to the bank to get a car loan for $3000. He was outraged to discover that the bank was only offering 8 percent Certificates of Deposit (CDs). *Only 8 percent.* Can you imagine?

Here's the thing: My grandfather's financial mantra *doesn't work anymore*. For a time, I believed his advice like gospel. I was lucky enough to learn though, that not much financial advice holds up for the long term, and that I need to constantly educate myself on new trends and advice in the field.

Unfortunately, these strategies didn't lead to the same success for the next generation. Trying to make their own successes required very different tactics and strategies for Grandpa Leroy's children, and from their example, I learned just how important it is to keep pace with the ever-evolving financial market. It's why I do what I do as a financial advisor. Of course, Grandpa wasn't maliciously extending poor advice. He taught what had worked for him. But it does not work today.

Many of today's retirees have similar stories. They watched their grandparents and parents retire with pensions and simple investments in CDs and government bonds. Some discover too late that it probably takes more to retire successfully in the twenty-first century. I often joke that Grandpa could afford to experiment and make mistakes. He hit the jackpot of financial climates. He retired with no debt, had an excellent pension, and lived during a seemingly ever-climbing market. In fact, the Dow Jones experienced over 1,000 percent growth for the duration of his retirement! If taxes were a bit heavy, or if broker dealer products included costly hidden fees, Leroy probably wouldn't have noticed. He could afford it. His children's generation is contending with different circumstances. They're squeezing for everything they can get. It's imperative to reduce unnecessary fees, minimize taxes, plan withdrawal order carefully, and be aware of the amount of risk they are taking. Whatever you can do to expand the longevity of your dollars, *do it*.

Retire Your Way

There are few things more tragic than finding that after decades in the workforce, the retirement we envisioned may not be within our reach. Even more heart-wrenching would be to reach the precipice of "guaranteed" financial security only to relapse on the cusp of retirement.

Every year, we host several client social events. Finance is deeply personal; a good, reputable financial advisor won't take a clinical approach to helping clients. It's important that an advisor and client establish mutual trust and to me, our client-staff events should blur the line between workplace acquaintances and friends. Many who attend our events have worked with us for years. It's always satisfying to look at the sea of clients and families and know we're helping many of them achieve their best financial situation possible. At one of our most recent get-togethers, I saw a couple whom we'll call Carl and Lizzy.

When I first met Carl, he was sixty-one. I told him what I tell all potential clients when we first meet: that the goal of meeting for the first time is so that people can experience how we help you make your own decisions through education and tools. As Carl would later put it, our job is to help clients "figure out how to get from their working days to their non-working days." The first interaction with an advisor or firm will set the tone for what clients can expect to experience every time they meet or need to evaluate a financial decision. Usually at the end of the second meeting we ask people just one question: "do you like the way we do things?" They don't need to make any investment decisions; they're simply deciding if they like the way we communicate and the tools we use. *Usually* that's how things work. But this was not how Carl and Lizzy came in for their first meeting. Instead, they walked through our doors in a veritable panic.

Carl had planned to retire in five years, at age sixty-six. He and Lizzy were building a new house. It was a fascinating project: They were building a "barndominium." In case you've never heard of that, a barndominium, as its name suggests, is part barn, part condominium. It has the aesthetic of a barn with the internals of a house. Thirty percent of Carl and Lizzy's barndominium was reserved for a woodshop. The building would sit on a few acres of land, which included a private fishing pond.

But Carl and Lizzy had a problem. Carl's employer had just informed him that he would likely be laid off in the next year. Imagine you're five years from retirement, you have a massive construction project underway, and suddenly your job of the past thirty-plus years is taken from you. Sadly, I see situations like Carl's regularly. Employers aren't supposed to discriminate, but ageism is real and prolific. Now Carl had important decisions to make. Would he abandon his building project to save some money? Did he need to find alternative employment, or could he get by on his investments? He and Lizzy had invested wisely over the years, but they didn't have a concrete retirement plan. That's how they found themselves in my office.

Our goal with clients like Carl and Lizzy is to get them to a place where—if and when that layoff comes—it won't matter. We're aiming to help them find financial stability without an employer, so that, whether they begin the job hunt (no small task after sixty) or embrace retirement, they won't have to sacrifice their lifestyle, their emotional stability, or their dreams (like Carl's "barndominium").

How do you picture retirement? Whatever the case, there's one thing of which you can be sure: It won't work if there aren't funds to support it. That may sound bleak, but it doesn't have to be. Carl and Lizzy were afraid because they were thrust into the unknown. An integrated plan, however, made all the difference in the world.

In this book, I'll cover several financial strategies that go into the making of a retirement plan. Some of the concepts and principles may seem foreign to you. The media often promotes confusing Wall Street jargon. You won't find that here. Instead, you'll read about time-tested and understandable methods that *make sense*. They probably won't match the retirement process that your parents and grandparents followed. That's good. Today's financial market is unique, and it behooves us to adjust our views of retirement. I urge you to approach the information with an open mind. You may be surprised even to find that ideas you thought were basic no longer hold merit in today's financial landscape.

My goal is to educate and inform. You'll learn about investment, wealth preservation, taxes, avoiding hidden fees, and more. My hope is that it will prepare you to make sound financial decisions that will contribute to the retirement of your dreams. The following material includes my opinion, but it is also based on years of research and study from experts in the finance and investment world. Retirement can feel overwhelming, but it doesn't need to be. With a good plan, you can enter retirement confident in your financial future. So, turn the page and let's get started. This is not your grandpa's retirement!

Chapter One
Who Is Today's Retiree?

I f you're familiar with Frisco, Texas, where I live and work, there's a good chance you've visited Cowboys Stadium in nearby Arlington, home of the Dallas Cowboys. Well, it's called AT&T stadium now. But fans still identify it by its original name. The stadium was built in 2009 and cost $1.3 billion to construct. That same year, the iconic jumbo screen that hovers above midfield was awarded the Guinness world record for largest high-definition video display in the world. We love our football in Texas, and a Cowboys game is the crème de la crème of the sport.

If you've been to a game, I'm sure you remember the magic of its atmosphere. Fans erupt into cheers as the team emerges from its locker room and takes the field. Chants ring out, honoring America's team. The game begins and the Cowboys set off. As the team drives downfield the crowd surges with energy. Eighty thousand people scream, "Let's go Cowboys!" between each down. When the Cowboys score a touchdown, the spectators' deafening roar is probably audible across all of Texas. After the game, as people shuffle back to their cars, you hear, "How 'bout them Cowboys?" echo faintly around the parking lot.

Have you got the setting clear in mind? Can you see the 80,000 cheering fans – an ocean of blue and white jerseys as far as the eye can see? Now, imagine every one of those people retiring within the week.

And not just this week. Picture a group almost that large retiring *every week* for the next ten years or more. That's where we stand in the United States right now. More than 10,000 people retire every day. History has never seen the likes. It makes sense, though, because today's retiree is a product of the Baby Boom.

What's a Baby Boomer?

The world was hopeful when the twentieth century rolled around, but things quickly turned for the worse. In 1914, a darkness settled over the world, punctuated with the outbreak of World War I. Not long thereafter came a second world war and again nations around the globe were cast into a frenzy. Unsurprisingly, the American psyche, and economy, was damaged for a time.

Then came the 1950s. In a way, it was the real beginning to America's twentieth century. Finally, the threat of global conflict was fading into the past. For decades, the American people had forgone normal lives. There hadn't been time to develop a career and raise a family when the greater good was at stake. By the time World War II ended in 1945, Americans had a lot to make up for.

Industrial plants which had churned out munitions were repurposed to mass produce household goods. There had been a technology boom in the early 1900s, but it only sustained an ever more sophisticated war strategy. Finally, modern technologies could improve the everyday life of average American people. Luxuries were becoming mainstream and technology had never been more accessible.

There's a basic fact of life: when times are good, people make babies. For more than thirty years, men had been spending their prime years across the sea. At last, they were at home with their families. In 1946, 3.4 million babies were born in the United States. In fact, October 1946 saw a 20 percent increase in live births (that's about nine months after World War II ended, in case you're wondering). Thus, began the "baby boom." The numbers would continue to climb over the next twenty-eight years, up to 1964, when the baby boomer generation is officially cut off. In that interim, the birth rate exceeded four million babies per year *every year*. By comparison, annual births in the United States have only exceeded four million thirteen times in the last twenty-eight years, the last time in 2009.[1]

In 1964, young baby boomers made up a staggering 40 percent of the American population. But they would be special for more than volume. Baby boomers would come to have a greater socioeconomic impact on the United States, and the world, than any generation before them.[2]

Baby boomers got their name for an obvious reason, the baby boom. Well, their parents' generation was also appropriately christened: The Silent Generation. Members of the Silent Generation grew up during the Great Depression. They learned early on that survival meant working hard and never complaining. Most of their formative years were spent in financial destitution. Then they were sent off to war. However, they returned to a world reborn. The federal government was eager to revitalize the American economy and homebound soldiers could expect several government incentives. During the war, unemployment had ended. Jobs were aplenty and money was flowing. Congress passed the G.I. Bill of rights which encouraged veterans to pursue higher education and expand into suburbia. The Silent Generation may have come from nothing, but they'd built a thriving economy and society by the time their children came along.

Baby boomers were thereby endowed with special privilege. They were born into thriving circumstances the likes of which America

---

[1] Erin Duffin. Statista. August 9, 2019. "Number of births in the United States from 1990 to 2017 (in millions)."
https://www.statista.com/statistics/195908/number-of-births-in-the-united-states-since-1990/
[2] History. 2019. "Baby Boomers." https://www.history.com/topics/world-war-ii/baby-boomers-video

hadn't seen in fifty years. But still, their parents engendered in them a work ethic born of Great Depression necessity. That made for a powerful combination. Baby boomers went on to make greater contribution to American society than any generation before. Even if we adjust for inflation, baby boomers are still the highest-earning generation in American history. They capitalized on their unique situation and thrived.

Now, that generation is retiring. It's hard to believe, right? If you'd expect that such an important (and large) generation's exodus from working life will dramatically affect the world, well, you'd be right. The implications are staggering. For the last fifty years or more, baby boomers have driven industry, revolutionized technology, broken down social borders, introduced civil liberties. This is the generation that tore down Jim Crow laws, thwarted communism, and put a man on the moon. They invented the internet for goodness' sake! Are they prepared to retire?

In short, not really.

In 2011, the first year that baby boomers started to retire, the Associated Press conducted a study to gauge how well boomers had equipped themselves. The results do not inspire confidence. In one prompt, baby boomers were asked to rate how confident they were that their financial preparedness would allow them to maintain their standard of life over the coming decades without a work income. Eighty-nine percent admitted to lacking confidence completely. Some 54 percent were sure they would need to work beyond age sixty-five to guarantee a comfortable retirement income. Another 67 percent said they might never stop working. Why? Not for love of work. Simply to afford the standard of living to which they'd grown accustomed.[3]

---

[3] Knowledge Networks. March 16, 2011. "Associated Press-Lifegoesstrong.com Boomers Survey."
http://surveys.associatedpress.com/data/KnowledgeNetworks/AP_Boomers_Surve y_Topline_RETIREMENT.pdf

You may be thinking, "2011 is a long time ago, surely baby boomers have figured out this retirement game by now." More recent studies would suggest otherwise. Research from the *Insured Retirement Institute* suggests that 45 percent of baby boomers have nothing saved for retirement.[4] *Nothing.* If nothing else, you might expect at least a 401(k) to provide *some* retirement income. The concept has been around since 1978, after all. Still, many boomers have not taken advantage of provisions like that to establish even a meager retirement nest egg.

Baby boomers are excellent earners. They work hard, and many earn substantial incomes. The problem, however, is that some boomers love to spend their money and they are often remiss to save it. Unlike their parents, most boomers have never had it so bad. They grew up in America's golden era. It was a consumer's paradise. They pioneered use of the credit card. Money was there to be made, and products were there to be bought. Saving was absent from the equation. Now, that "spend first, save later" propensity is finally catching up.

Living Too Long?

There's another problem facing today's retiree: people are just living too long. Okay, so that's not really a *problem*. Living longer sounds great but let me explain what I mean.

First, it's without question that people are living longer these days than generations past. The Urban Institute, which tracks census figures, found that life expectancy at birth jumped nearly twenty years between baby boomers and their parents. Additionally, people turning sixty-five in 2030 can expect to outlive their parents by six or more years. Do you know what the fastest growing age group is in the

---

[4] Insured Retirement Institute. April 2019. "Boomer Expectations for Retirement 2019."
https://www.myirionline.org/docs/default-source/default-document-library/iri_babyboomers_whitepaper_2019_final.pdf?sfvrsn=0

United States? It's not working aged people, and it's not children. It's the eighty-five-and-older population. Some estimates purport that, by 2050, Americans eighty-five or older will make up as large a percentage of our total population as did people sixty-five and older in 1930. Well that's good news! We're living much longer than our parents and grandparents before us. But, living longer means that your retirement savings need to last longer too—and sometimes that's easier said than done.[5]

Outliving one's money is a common concern. In fact, it's many baby boomers' greatest concern of all. Greater than insects, snakes, heights, drowning is the concern that boomers "won't have enough money to afford retirement," reports *MarketWatch,* a finance website operated by the Dow Jones. The report continues, "43 percent of those interviewed [by the Transamerica Center for Retirement Studies] said their greatest fear about retirement was outliving their savings and investments. This fear surpassed [...] even death."

A survey, conducted by the American Institute of CPAs and cited in the same *MarketWatch* article, corroborates that conclusion. This time, financial planners were polled and asked to identify the number one concern among their clients. Fifty-seven percent answered that "running out of money was the top retirement concern for their clients." Clearly, the way we think of retirement needs adjustment.[6]

Will Social Security Be There?

Let me make something clear right away—Social Security will be there for you. If you're nearing retirement you've probably heard a lot to suggest otherwise. Unfortunately, many negative reports come with an

[5] Accounting Degree Review. 2019. "The Crisis in Pensions and Retirement Plans." https://www.accounting-degree.org/retirement/
[6] Catey Hill. MarketWatch. July 21, 2019. "Older people fear this more than death." https://www.marketwatch.com/story/older-people-fear-this-more-than-death-2016-07-18

agenda, and they're not necessarily backed with evidence. Social Security does have some obstacles to overcome in the next several decades, however. The following is some history and the *facts* about where Social Security stands today.

Social Security was introduced in 1935. It was part of President Franklin D. Roosevelt's New Deal. It established sixty-five as the magic number for retirement, the age at which Americans first qualified to collect the new government funded retirement income. Ironically, though, in 1935 the life expectancy for men barely surpassed fifty-nine. Women were fortunate enough to reach sixty-three. Either way, the average American would never live to see Social Security benefits. As we've already made clear, that does not apply to today's retiree.[7]

In the next forty years, a whopping 20 percent of the American population will consist of people sixty-five and over. As of 2017, about 23 percent of the population is made up of children. That means that if we look at just the working age demographic of the United States, nearly 30 percent will not be working in coming decades. Thirty percent of a nation's adults *will not be part of its workforce.* That's shocking when you really think about it. In 1950, assuming you made it to sixty-five and could retire, your Social Security check would be funded by the taxes of sixteen American workers. With the retired population saturating, that ratio dropped to 3.3 workers per retiree in 2010, and it's only getting worse. It is predicted that by 2025, each Social Security beneficiary will have only two workers sustaining his or her check.[8]

Already, the United States government has been devoting huge amounts of money to sustain Social Security. In 2011, President Barack Obama budgeted 3.8 trillion dollars for government spending. Fifty-seven percent of that, or 2.2 trillion dollars, was spent in Social

---

[7] Allianz Life of North America. "Rethinking what's ahead in retirement." https://www.allianzlife.com/-/media/files/allianz/documents/ent_1154_n.pdf

[8] ChildStats.com. September 2018. "Pop2 Children as a Percentage of the Population." https://www.childstats.gov/americaschildren/tables/pop2.asp

Security payments. That makes sense considering that 35 percent of American retirees rely entirely on Social Security. It also makes sense why Social Security funds are running out. Since 2010, Social Security has paid more to retirees than it's been funded.

It's no wonder, then, that people are concerned. Sixty percent of working Americans worry that Social Security will have dried up by the time they are old enough to qualify. Of those already retired, 56 percent have said they expect to lose benefits before they die. Their apprehension is understandable, but, I believe, premature. I hear some so-called experts in my field preaching that Social Security is a goner and retirees might as well abandon ship. If someone tells you that, give it about five minutes before they start pushing a product. Social Security is facing some challenges, but it's a myth that the system will go broke or declare bankruptcy in the near future. As things stand now, Social Security benefits are relatively "safe" until about 2090, and that's if Congress does nothing to boost the system. But Congress knows who the voters are; it won't be quick to slash the voting generation's benefits. If you're a member of the baby boomer generation like most of my clients, I'm not concerned that you won't have Social Security benefits. I can't, however, say that for your children.[9]

That said, there is little reason to fear that Social Security will completely falter. In fact, this isn't even the first time that people have exaggerated the severity of its condition. In the 1980s, Social Security came close to depleting its reserves, but Congress made some policy adjustments which promptly restored the program's dependability. It's been nearly forty years since finance "experts" condemned Social Security back then and yet the program is still running strong. Funny how that works, right?[10]

---

[9] Accounting Degree Review. 2019. "The Crisis in Pensions and Retirement Plans." https://www.accounting-degree.org/retirement/

[10] Eileen Ambrose. AARP. 2018. "Six More Myths About Social Security." https://www.aarp.org/retirement/social-security/info-2016/debunking-six-more-myths-about-social-security.html

The Value of Social Security

Now that I've explained some of the realistic challenges facing Social Security, let me tell you why I still consider it an essential facet of any retirement portfolio.

Social Security is one of the few inflation-adjusted incomes left for retirees. In other words, the Social Security Administration accounts for what's called the "cost-of-living adjustment." On average, we might estimate that prices increase by at least two percent annually. Of course, the real number varies from year to year. In 2017 it was a low .98 percent. In 2018, the inflation rate rose to 2 percent. At the time of this book's writing, the number sits at 2.7 percent. It's safe to estimate that inflation could rise by closer to 3 percent every year.

At first thought, 2 to 3 percent inflation doesn't sound that bad. At three percent inflation, a $1 loaf of bread will cost $1.03 in a year. That hardly appears dramatic. But inflation is insidious. It slowly chips away at the value of our money. And inflation is a form of compounding interest. For example, if inflation doubles the cost of living in twenty years, the value of a million dollars in a bank account today will be effectively cut in half twenty years into one's retirement.

Hopefully it's clear, then, just how valuable an inflation adjusted income source can be for a retiree. Often, the way you claim your Social Security benefit can have a powerful impact on the longevity and sustainability of your other retirement income vehicles. The more inflation adjusted income you have, the better prepared you'll be to contend with the on-going risk of inflation. In turn, you'll be better able to maintain your lifestyle throughout retirement.

When I was growing up in the 1970s, our family's home was lined with cringe-inducing brown and orange flower pattern wallpaper (forgive my parents; that style was "hip" at the time). When we sold the house in the 1990s, it had the same dreadful décor. Now imagine if a retired couple bought the house and to this day, they lived in that brown Hawaiian shirt of a home because they couldn't afford to make any updates on their fixed income with its waning value?

All right, so that example may sound funnier than it does alarming, but the underlying principle is sound. If soon-to-be retirees don't plan for inflation, they may be forced to adjust their standard of living over the course of retirement. That would be disappointing because, in most cases, it's unnecessary. Wise use of your Social Security benefit is often enough to help protect against the corrosive influence of inflation.

Survivor's Benefit

A second valuable aspect of Social Security is the "survivor's benefit." If you're married, and you and your spouse both collect Social Security benefits, guess what happens when one spouse passes away? The survivor will continue to collect *the larger* of the two benefits. In other words, you lose one benefit.

Many people entering retirement only think about the expenses they have *today* and their Social Security benefit as it stands *today*. But what will happen when that benefit is reduced? I challenge people to think beyond today's needs and consider the impact of how large or small that survivor's benefit may be. Looking at an analysis of your total expected lifetime Social Security benefit can help you, but that method is limited; it omits other relevant information. This information is highly specific to you—details like when you will stop working, the percentage of your expenses covered by Social Security benefits, and inflation assumptions, just to name a few. To be fully informed when you make your Social Security claiming decision, you need to consider this "survivor's benefit" size in the plan. I call this the "spousal continuation plan."

The way you coordinate your Social Security benefit with your spouse can make a lasting impact on your retirement. If you or your spouse predeceases the other by some time, having carefully arranged your withdrawal procedure can make the difference of many thousands of dollars in subsequent years.

When couples are flippant about coordinating their Social Security benefits, I often think of a friend and client of mine who we'll call Rob. One day while the two of us were reviewing Rob's finances together, I noticed an unusual expense. "Rob," I asked, "What's this '$267 to mom?'"

"Well," Rob said, "It's been hard on my mom since my dad passed so my brothers and I are helping to make up the difference."

As it turned out, Rob and his brothers were pooling their money to make up for an $800 deficit in their mother's retirement. I listened in a stupor as Rob explained how dire her situation had become. I knew his mother and her circumstances going into retirement. Her financial condition should never have gotten so bad.

Rob's mother and father, whom we'll call Eric and Diane, retired from a factory in Oklahoma when they were both sixty-two. They did what most people do—they claimed their Social Security benefits right away. That was probably the first mistake. Years later, Rob's parents were living exclusively off their Social Security benefit. Their retirement savings dried up faster than expected. Still, things weren't so bad. Their house was paid off, so they managed to save about $300 a month. Eric collected about $2,500 a month and Diane received $1,250.

What the family didn't know was that Eric had prostate cancer. He'd had it for some time, but it went undetected. By the time Eric visited a doctor, the cancer was severe. In eighteen months, he passed away.

The survivor's benefit meant Diane collected her husband's $2,500 per month after his death, but it wasn't enough. She quickly burned through what little savings the couple had accrued in recent years.

Finally, she was forced to do what she swore she never would—ask her sons for help.

After some quick calculations, I figured that if Eric and Diane had not taken their full Social Security benefit at sixty-two and used a "restricted" strategy instead, Diane would have been left with about $3,300 a month after she lost her husband. That would have accounted for exactly the deficit that she now required from her boys.

Now, the restricted strategy was altered in 2015 with the Bipartisan Budget Reduction Act. However, if a retiree has not claimed Social Security and he or she was born before 1954, they are still entitled to the restricted strategy. It also exists for the widows and widowers of deceased "number holders."

This is why it's so important for any pre-retiree or retiree to look into getting professional advice. There are many people who have no idea how many options they might have, and how many decisions they can actually make in order to prepare for a brighter retirement.

An Insider Look At Social Security

The Program Operations Manual System (POMS) is the procedure manual for Social Security Administration (SSA) workers. Most of it is overcomplicated, in my view, but there are at least three important things we can learn from this insider source:

1. Social Security employees are specifically prohibited from giving you advice about how to take your benefit. They can confirm questions and assumptions you have, but they will not be able to give you a breakdown of the various ways you can take a benefit, and which one gives you the highest check over time.

2. SSA workers cannot elaborate on the various options you will have. Unless you ask about specific ways to coordinate benefits, they will not proactively inform you if you qualify for spousal benefits, ex-spouse benefits, or benefits for a deceased spouse.

3. SSA workers cannot give you advice about how to coordinate your benefit with your other retirement savings. Should you spend your retirement savings now and defer your Social Security benefit until later? Or should you preserve your retirement savings and instead take your Social Security benefit sooner? The answer to this question is unique to your situation, and a Social Security employee is not equipped—or permitted—to give you an answer. It's not as simple as an "early or late" decision. *When* you choose to withdraw Social Security has a more significant impact on your cumulative retirement plan than you may realize.

Now, don't get me wrong; I am not saying that Social Security employees aren't interested in your financial well-being. But their job isn't to plan for the entirety of your retired life. In my experience, many retirees will need additional help to claim their benefits in the most advantageous way. In my office, we use a special software that helps us to strategize with the big picture in mind. Because of the multiple possible scenarios and moving numbers, software is tremendously helpful. It's important to view different financial decisions through different lenses. Software that simulates different outcomes can help families make their best decisions.

Getting your own personalized analysis for Social Security is straightforward and simple. To get started, you will typically need just your benefit amount and a little personal information, like when you plan to stop working and your birthday. You can request a Social Security analysis as a standalone report, or it can be combined with a more integrated plan. I'll talk more about an integrated plan later when I go over what I call the "Money Master Retirement Plan".

I appreciate the software. Humans can't always account for every variable, but a computer can. In fact, if I didn't use a timing software, there's a chance I'd be dropping the ball, keeping potential money away from some families.

Ultimately, we cannot rely on anyone but ourselves to fund our retirement life. Social Security is an important piece of the puzzle, but more is required to complete your retirement picture. It is our responsibility to plan wisely during our working years so that we can live comfortably for many future decades. The next chapter will examine some ideas about how that planning process should work.

Chapter One Key Lessons

- The longevity problem can be improved by optimizing Social Security for your situation.
- Social Security provides inflation adjustments.
- The survivor benefit amount should be considered for every married couple.
- Special Social Security optimization software can help test various combinations to discover which claiming strategy is right for you.

Chapter Two
Planning for The Modern Era

April 24, 1912. The frigid waters of the North Atlantic Ocean were still and calm. To passengers and crew aboard the RMS Titanic, life was good, and the sailing was smooth. Little did they know the danger that lay in wait along their fateful course.

"Iceberg right ahead!" Rang out the panicked warning at 11:40 p.m. The ship's lookout was frantic as he identified the hazard. An iceberg hovered in the ship's path. Although most of the iceberg was under water, its mass exceeded the Titanic's by ten times—easily enough to gut the vessel and sink it.

By three in the morning on April 25, the Titanic had been wretched in two. Its halves were sinking into the icy depths above a two-mile trench. It would eventually come to rest along the ocean bed along with some 1500 passengers.

Only twenty-five minutes into this ordeal, Captain Edward J. Smith knew that the Titanic would not survive. He gave the order for lifeboats to be prepared and lowered into the sea with women and children. "How could this be happening?" he surely thought. The Titanic was, after all, unsinkable!

As the lifeboats cast off, a glaring dilemma became apparent: There would not be enough space for all the passengers. The ship was designed to carry thirty-two lifeboats, each with a seventy-person

15

capacity, enough room for the 2224 passengers aboard. However, only twenty lifeboats were on board. The Oceanic Steam Navigation Company, the shipping company that owned Titanic, had made an executive decision to remove more than a third of its safety rafts to permit better views of the ocean. After all, what does an unsinkable ship need emergency rafts for, right?

To make the disaster even worse, most of the twenty lifeboats departed at about half capacity making the final survival number 710, just 32 percent of the passengers. What had gone wrong? How could such a catastrophic disaster befall the greatest accomplishment of maritime engineering at the time?

Failure to recognize risk.

Planning is everything. It was a lack of planning—a failure to look into the true risk—that contributed most to the Titanic's downfall. To declare a ship "unsinkable" was reckless. Sure, she was constructed from the finest steel manufacturable at the time. Yeah, she had a double bottom and there were fifteen distinct sections that could be sealed individually to cut off the spreading of water in the event of a hull breach. Impressive features in the ship's advertisements, but they meant little to the iceberg. Arrogance marked every step in the Titanic's journey, from construction to its christening, departure, voyage, and untimely demise.

Overconfidence Killed the Cat

Wait, is that how the saying goes? Well, it should. Being unaware of what their portfolio maximum drawdown looks like is one of the most troubling things I see in soon-to-be retirees when they come into our office. Some who come into my office already have a plan, but it's incomplete or insufficient. I'll talk about the risks of that scenario later in this chapter.

As I'm writing this book in 2019, the economic crashes of 2008 (and 2000, remember that?) are nearly all but faded from the collective memory. For people who lost up to half of their life's investments in the Great Recession it's a different story. The pain is still fresh in mind. For some, they've only recently recovered everything they lost a decade ago.

Now, don't get me wrong. The economy is doing well now. Since the Great Recession concluded, there have been ten years of no bear markets. Positivity has returned to the market, and the Wall Street guys are riding high.

So, what similarity is there between what happened to the Titanic and people today?

Things are going well, and thus many turn a blind eye to risk. Not being aware of risk—not understanding the worst-case scenario—is one of the aging investor's worst enemies.

In 2008, things were going well too, and I believe that it blinded many of the smartest investors. Overconfidence led banks to haphazardly hand out mortgage loans. It seems like a joke, looking back now, just how easy it was to get a loan. In some cases, you didn't even need to prove eligibility! Major banks were "too big to fail," so why did it matter? That was until Lehman Brother Inc., one of the world's largest investment banking companies, filed for bankruptcy. Nearly a dozen others of those "major banks" came within inches of following suit. Thus, popped what became known as the housing bubble. The stock market crash followed shortly thereafter.

You probably have noticed the similarity between the 2008 market crisis and the Titanic's devastation in 1912. 'Twas overconfidence killed the beast. I believe that arrogance inspired the overconfidence, mostly on the part of big companies and investing giants like Lehman Brothers. Sadly, however, it was the unknowing individual investors who suffered the most. Often, they could not read the market themselves, and they were misled by supposed experts who oversold their prophetic ability. The stock market is unpredictable, and that fact will remain regardless of any financial fortune-teller's claims to the contrary.

I wouldn't say that today's investors are "arrogant." Many, however, are similar to the Titanic patrons. They are overconfident in the amount of risk they are taking, and they aren't aware that there ought to be more safety rafts on board!

I remember talking to an older couple in 2008—family friends. They'd always done well for themselves. This couple, whom we'll call the Bernards, owned a small real estate company which they had planned to hand over to their son who worked for the firm. Then everything went wrong.

"Our broker told us that our investment portfolio was diversified," the wife said. "We knew we might lose a bit, but about 40 percent of our net worth disappeared, it seems, overnight."

When the stock market fell, the Bernards were sixty-five and sixty-three. They had personal savings just north of $500,000, which they had invested in a brokerage account. It was their "guaranteed retirement income," because, like their broker had said, those assets were diversified. In other words, they were supposed to be completely "safe."

Let's just pause here for a moment. I cringe when I hear potential clients tell me that their investment portfolio is "diversified" in a brokerage account, because the term is misleading. Diversification is essential to investment, but the word is often misused. Yes, your money may be stored in several different investment vehicles (often mutual funds). But with a poorly organized and un-unified investment plan, those mutual funds may have the same holdings as other accounts within the portfolio. With a rather simple portfolio stress test, you can identify overlap between different accounts within your investment portfolio, but most people don't know how to do that. When the stock market tanks, it doesn't matter that your broker has allocated your money into five different options—it's all going down.

You're led to believe that if the stock market dips, maybe one fifth of your money will take a hit. That's what the Bernards thought.

The Bernards had planned to retire within a few years. But, by December 2008, their $500,000 had dropped to $300,000. Every day, it lost a little bit more. Their retirement hopes were shattered.

"Our broker is telling us to just hang in there and it will eventually come back up," the wife continued. They were hoping that I'd have a different solution to their money problem. Unfortunately, at that point, their broker was right. There was no magic reset button to recover lost assets. Safety measures should have been taken long before the market crash to better protect their retirement income.

Three Phases of Financial Life

The Bernards may have planned better if they'd understood the three phases of financial life. Bad timing often equates to investing according to the wrong phase of your life. Let me explain. The three phases are:

- Accumulation
- Preservation
- Distribution

The **accumulation phase** is for young people, young being about ages twenty to fifty. When we begin to work as an adult, we've begun the accumulation phase. Our investment goal is to make as much money as we can and save, save, save. In the accumulation phase we can typically afford to take higher risk. To make as much money as possible, we usually employ more aggressive investment strategies. Naturally, that means that we accept a higher risk of loss. But that's okay, since timing is on our side. If we lose money in a market downturn, it's not the end of the world. We're still working and living off our income. We have time for the market to potentially recover, to regain our assets, and even acquire more.

Eventually, however, we need to adjust our perception of risk. As we near retirement, we should reprioritize such that preservation is a higher priority. Unsurprisingly, we call this the **preservation phase.** It normally lasts about ten to fifteen years and concludes with your retirement. Defining the phases of financial life isn't complicated. The function and purpose of these phases is simple, but difficulty lies in adherence to the appropriate strategies of each.

A big problem I see is people missing the transition from the accumulation phase to the preservation phase. It's an easy and understandable mistake, but it can be a problem. Subjecting ourselves to high risk as we near retirement is just plain risky. That's what happened to the Bernards. Their investment style was befitting much younger people. It was especially easy to neglect the risk because it was the result of company stocks which had been given them. Many investors have similar situations. They unknowingly tolerate high risk from stocks that skew their portfolio in the wrong direction. It's not until an economic scare comes along that some realize the risks in their planning style, or until they read a book that warns about it (hint hint).

The accumulation phase is *risky*. But that's okay when we have the *time* to afford higher risk. In our later working years, it's essential that we make changes to our investment protocol.

The **distribution phase** is simple. That's after we've retired and we're living on sources of income which we've developed over the course of our working lives. The distribution phase is our time to rest and enjoy the fruits of our labor, that is, if we've done everything right in the first two stages of our financial lives. Some investment is still important, but strictly with a view to growth potential and lower risk. Investment strategies must be conservative because we can't afford to lose our finite resources. Without regular income, our capacity to produce obviously diminishes.

A Rule of 100?

Many older financial planners promote something called the Rule of 100. It goes something like this: Let's say that you're sixty years old. If we subtract your age from one hundred, we arrive at your risk tolerance as a percentage of total assets. In other words, at sixty years old, you can afford to have 40 percent of your money invested in equities, as opposed to less risky assets like bonds. As a "rule of thumb," the principle endures. Here's the problem, though: traditionally, financial advisors have suggested that what remains of your assets should be housed safely in bonds. It's true that bonds are considered a "safe option," and, thirty years ago, when most financial advisors were cutting their teeth and the Rule of 100 was conceived, that wasn't bad advice. Unfortunately, that advice is outmoded today.

Thirty years ago, bonds were not only considered "safer", but they offered tremendous growth potential as a non-stock option. Unfortunately, in today's economic climate, bonds afford little room for growth. Interest rates at the time of this book's writing are at an all-time low. It's not that bonds aren't still a reasonably conservative investment, nor that I don't think they may be a wise option in later years. But, right now, bonds aren't necessarily the safe haven they used to be in today's financial environment and their value often pales in comparison to modern investment vehicles

The 4 Percent Rule

While we're on outdated financial principles, it's worth mentioning the 4 percent rule—another retirement guideline that's been thrown around over the years to which many a retiree has subscribed.

About forty years ago, a financial planner named William P. Bengen devised the four percent rule. His objective was to determine the ideal percentage of a brokerage account that one could annually withdraw in retirement and not run out for thirty years—the retirement sweet spot, so to speak.[11]

It was an ambitious undertaking. Withdrawal strategy is one of the most important and potentially stressful retirement decisions retirees need to make. If you take out too much, you risk depleting your retirement funds prematurely. Conversely, withdrawing too little robs us a higher living standard. How great would it be if it was as simple as withdrawing a flat four percent each year? Unfortunately, it's not that easy and there isn't a magic number.

When Bengen published his "4 percent rule" (later it would be determined that 4.5 was, in fact, more accurate) the stock market was soaring, and the economy looked like it'd never drop off. According to that standard, Bengen's rule worked swimmingly. However, when the tech bubble burst in 2000 and everything went south, a simplistic application of the four percent rule began to manifest some problems. Following the market crash of 2000, it would take about ten years for the economy to see an appreciable gain. Economic conditions remained so stagnant that experts have retroactively dubbed 2000 to 2010 the "lost decade."

It's not that the four percent rule is inherently flawed. But it's not as simple in practice as many would-be investors contend. While 4 percent is still a sound baseline, withdrawal percentage must consider other factors like equities to bond ratio, inflation adjustments, and rules to correct portfolio fluctuation.

Here's the problem I see all too often, though. In today's day and age, most of us are quick to consult Google whenever we need help, even in deciding how to make major life decisions. So, as people approach retirement, they google something like "retirement strategies." A series of articles pop up quoting supposed finance experts who recommend strategies like the 4 percent rule or the Rule

---

[11] Sean McDonnell. Kiplinger. January 25, 2018. "Why the 4% Withdrawal Rule Is Wrong." https://www.kiplinger.com/article/retirement/T037-C032-S014-why-the-4-withdrawal-rule-is-wrong.html

of 100 or basic suggestions about CDs and annuities. Those sound pretty good. So, people end up self-prescribing. They develop something of a retirement plan based on the "research" they found on the internet. But how effective do you think that plan will really be?

Imagine walking into a pharmacy and rattling off to the pharmacist a list of medicines that you need for your various health conditions. The pharmacist asks you for a prescription from your doctor, but you don't have one. "But I did all my own research online," you protest, "I don't need a doctor's prescription. Do you think the pharmacist will then concede and give you whatever you want? Of course not! That would be ridiculous. Why do medications require doctor prescriptions in the first place? It's not just to prevent people from abusing certain drugs; it's to protect even sincere patients from further damaging their health from the misuse of powerful medicine.

Why then are people so quick to "self-prescribe" when it comes to the financial world?

A financial plan is a process of examining and evaluating potential decisions through multiple lenses. Everyone needs such a plan, and it is more involved than Google would lead you to believe. All money spends better with a written and up to date plan. If you're afraid that you may not be successful in retirement, then I believe you need an up-to-date, written plan to make every penny count. If you are not afraid of retirement because you feel that you are quite well off, you too might want a written and up-to-date plan. It can help you to spend your money to its maximum potential.

The 4 percent rule was not flawed in concept, but too many Google-searching, soon-to-be retirees have incorrectly applied it. It's also important to know that this so-called perfect formula to a successful retirement does not take into account the long life of many retirees. Because our life expectancy is so much higher than others at the time of the 4 percent rule's conception, some of us often forget that the math might not check out the same way it did at another time.

The biggest mistake I see people make with respect to the 4 percent rule and other common retirement strategies is neglecting to account for the many factors involved in successful execution. Some factors are that the 4 percent rule was developed before the Great Recession, during a time in which stocks were at all-time highs, riding the dot-com bubble. Another reason: it fails to account for lengthening lifespans that place a higher demand on retirement assets. Another factor: Inflation.

Inflation, Does It Matter?

Inflation used to be the nation's bogeyman. It was always a concern, but no one seemed to really understand how it worked or what it meant for their finances.

In 1974, Gerald Ford assumed the presidency, having inherited it from his notorious predecessor, Richard Nixon. President Ford was bequeathed a nation in financial tatters. America was enduring its greatest economic crisis since the Great Depression. Inflation had risen to 12.3 percent following 1973's oil crisis. In response, Ford launched a campaign called "Whip Inflation Now." The "WIN" buttons became an unusual talisman of the 1970s. Ford hoped that the movement would inspire the American people to manage their own money more responsibly and thereby improve the nation's collective inflation problem. But what did inflation mean for the average American? And does it matter to us now?[12]

Inflation is not exactly the looming monster that the WIN campaign advertised. It's more like an insidious parasite that strikes imperceptibly. Nonetheless its effects are felt. Inflation, normally

---

[12]Amy Farber. Federal Reserve Bank of New York. July 13, 2012. "Historical Echoes: Whip Inflation Now ... and Then."
https://libertystreeteconomics.newyorkfed.org/2012/07/historical-echoes-whip-inflation-now-and-then.html

represented as a percentage, is an increasing of prices for the same product. It matters to us because that means that the purchasing power of our money decreases.

Sadly, inflation doesn't care that you've retired. Let's say that at the time of your retirement, $80,000 is your minimum survivable annual income. You have a cool $2.4 million saved away to get you through the next thirty years. Is that enough? It would be if you only needed $80,000 a year for the rest of your life. But in twenty years you might need as much as $160,000. Even at a reasonable 2 percent rate of inflation, money can run out quickly. Our retirement plans need to account for inflation. There is no way around it.

Do you remember going to the movies as a kid? What did a ticket cost at the time? Depending on how far back you go, it may have cost a dollar or less. These days, it's more like $16. That's inflation. The same principle applies to gasoline, groceries, automobiles, housing—Everything for which you need money.

Inflation includes a second, possibly sinister roadblock: it's unpredictable. Inflation may be low now, but remember, in the 1970s it exceeded 10 percent. We can't say with absolute confidence what it will do in the future. Inflation will always remain an unknown factor. The best we can do is plan for the worst. I typically recommend that we use at least 3.2 percent as an assumed inflation rate is. I was recently at Subway and it cost $31 for two footlong sandwiches, a six-inch sandwich, chips, and drinks. My wife commented that it's become so much more expensive even within the last few years. When you are retired, and the cost of Subway goes up, you should be able to afford the increase without worrying that your long-term financial health is in jeopardy. Subway shouldn't feel like a "real treat!"[13]

It's a challenge to guarantee a long-lasting income with so many unknown variables floating around, but it's possible.

---

[13] Walter J. Williams. October 10, 2019. Shadow Government Statistics. "Alternate Inflation Charts." http://www.shadowstats.com/alternate_data/inflation-charts

Modern-Day Investment

Being uninformed and failing to plan can be major retirement gaffes. But, planning the wrong way—with old-fashioned standards like the Rule of 100 and blindly following the 4 Percent Rule—could just as effectively undermine your retirement.

It's a mistake to think that retirement strategies which worked for our parents and grandparents still apply in the twenty-first century. Remember, this is not your grandpa's retirement! You wouldn't expect a car from 1985 to match the performance and reliability of one made with modern technology. Neither should you expect decades-old advice to meet the requirements of today's retirement landscape.

As we approach retirement, our investment style needs to change. Otherwise we risk falling short of our retirement goals. In our final working years, focus shifts to preservation. We need dependable, sustainable income for decades of non-working life. That's not a small task, but it is achievable.

A Modern Method

It's hard to make major financial decisions that might alter the course of our retirement. Sometimes it feels overwhelming. I get it. Small decisions are much easier; individual purchases, for example. Say you wanted to buy a new TV. To decide if that purchase is financially responsible, you would first account for necessary expenses in your budget and then evaluate whether you have enough expendable income to cover the TV's price. If you don't, you might save until you can afford the TV without accruing unnecessary debt.

Bigger financial decisions should be assessed similarly. Average consumers often have difficulty making apples to apples comparisons. It's hard to compare added expenses, Social Security timing, pension settlement choice, relocating your home to a different size and place, different portfolios with different amounts of risk, timing of work stop date, taking a lesser paying but more fulfilling job and more. The first step in evaluating heavy decisions it to establish an advanced "budget" of sorts—a thorough and inclusive financial plan that lays out your financial snapshot. It should include current spending trends, earnings, taxes, inflation, savings rate, average return, variation from the average return, medical budget, vacation budget, health care, mortgage. All of this and more in a written and simulated plan. With such a plan, investors can see results in advance. It's easier to make decisions because you can see exactly what effect your choices will have on every facet of your retired life. As new decisions arise, it becomes easier to gauge your spending capacity by comparing potential adjustments to your financial plan. It's especially easy to do with modern software; plug in the numbers and the program will update to show your modified financial picture and let you know how you're doing. Difficult decisions are rendered simple. Did the decision improve your plan or not? If it improved your retirement income and afforded you more money over the next several decades, then go for it! Otherwise, it's probably best to adhere to your current plan.

The Money Master Retirement Plan

Financial planning has become somewhat synonymous with stock and bond investment. Some "financial planners" are just salesman in disguise and are not true fiduciaries. They gather assets, invest them in stocks and bonds, meet with clients once or twice a year, and then earn their commission. That is *not*, however, what a real financial advisor or planner does. If your financial *planner's* services don't include an integrated *plan*, it might be time to move on from your current advisor.

As you approach retirement, you probably have questions about things like Social Security timing, health care planning, tax efficiency, and estate planning strategies. Just like a doctor tests and analyzes your health through different lenses to prescribe the best medicine for your needs, a financial advisor is equipped to recommend a purpose-built process designed to fit your retirement needs. Many broker-dealer representatives are not. Over the years, we've identified five key areas in which soon-to-be retirees need high level advice. Brindle & Bay Wealth Management carefully devised the Money Master Retirement Plan™ process to address each one with a specific plan:

1. Income Distribution Plan
2. Investment Plan
3. Tax Optimized Plan
4. Health Care Plan
5. Legacy Plan

Do you know how often a potential client has come into my office with an income distribution plan from their last advisor? Almost never. Instead, they come in with a jumbled mess of transaction statements. Sometimes they have annuity illustrations that show how much money they can expect from certain assets. But a complete income plan? I've seen that maybe twice. And yet, income distribution is the number one concern I hear among people nearing retirement. They want to know how to maximize their withdrawals without prematurely expending their assets.

An income distribution plan communicates how money will be distributed over coming years and it outlines a withdrawal procedure that helps to maximize potential earning. After we put together the income distribution plan, we provide a "proof of concept" with customized software that outlines fair and reasonable assumptions so that you can trust that you have transparent assessment.

The other plans that comprise our Money Master Retirement Plan likewise work to ensure that every aspect of your retirement finances is optimized and protected. And, they are designed to combat the many investor challenges unique to today's retiring generation. The next chapter will examine some of these challenges.

Chapter Two Key Lessons:

• Examine your total true risk via a portfolio stress test.

• Identify the phase of financial life that you're in.

• Begin de-risking your portfolio if necessary

• Plan to give yourself raises during retirement.

• Do not "self-prescribe" through ideas like the 4 percent rule or the Rule of 100.

• Remember that a financial plan is a process, much like that used by a qualified doctor. Consider using a more modern model-tested technique to help you feel good about improving and organizing your retirement plan. Seeing how your plan responds in times of market strain can set your mind at ease when it comes to execution.

Chapter Three
Today's Retirement Challenges

D o you know what a truism is? It's a bit different than a truth. It's *true* that McDonald's once made bubble-gum flavored broccoli, that armadillo shells are bulletproof, and that there's a way to make water *wetter*. But those truths aren't obvious, and I bet you're curious to learn more about each one (sorry, you'll have to look them up yourself). A truism, on the other hand, is a truth so glaringly apparent, so laughably self-evident, that it's not worth saying. Truisms include cliché phrases like, "you get what you pay for," and, "you can't win them all." Authors are vilified for including truisms in their writing, but I'm going to use one anyway:

What goes up must come down.

Did you roll your eyes? I wouldn't be surprised, that's the reaction truisms normally incite. "What goes up must come down" is so obvious that I wonder how it took humans until 1687 to theorize the notion of gravity. But sometimes truisms are *too* obvious. We pay them no mind until an apple falls and smacks us in the head.

That seems to be the case in economics. Time and again, we've seen economies rise and fall; what goes up *always* comes down. And yet, governments, economists, and investors often fail to learn from this fundamental principle of economics.

Since the Great Depression, the United States has experienced about thirteen economic recessions. They've all paled in scale compared to the Great Depression of the 1930s, but they've followed the same pattern. First, the financial market soars to what seem like new heights. Investors are in good spirit and optimism runs high. Then, it all comes crashing down. America is not the only country to have suffered major economic setbacks in recent decades, though.

In the 1960s, Japan's economy was on the rise. By the 1970s, Japan had the second largest gross national product in the world, topped only by the United states, the population of which exceeds Japan's almost thirty-fold. In the 1980s, things started to get out of control.

Economies crash when product valuations far exceed their intrinsic values. A speculative market develops. The over-valuation of securities usually starts in the stock market as investors allow their excitement over new products to inflate share prices. Price inflation eventually permeates the larger economy including investment options like bonds, commodities, currencies, fine art, collectibles, and real estate. A sharp disconnect from reality ensues and it takes a market downturn to reestablish balance. At the peak of Japan's economic bubble, real estate prices had skyrocketed so quickly that in just a few years' time, a three-square meter area (ten square feet) by the Imperial Palace sold for a whopping $600,000. Can you imagine? What can you even do with a 10-by-10 postage stamp of land?

Japan's Finance Ministry eventually realized that its market conditions were unsustainable. To stem speculation, it raised interest rates. The stock market crashed immediately. Stockholders found themselves having invested heavily in assets which were now valueless. The worst part, however, was that many people invested with borrowed money. As they failed to make payments on their loans, a debt crisis developed. Finally, the banks themselves could no longer stay afloat having over-expended their lending capacities. Many consolidated to avoid bankruptcy while others relied on government bailouts.

Japan's Lost Decade

The resulting economic recession in Japan would last about ten years. Economists have come to call it Japan's "lost decade." The economy's decline eventually halted, but it could not resume growth. Low growth and deflation (yes, deflation can be just as bad as inflation) stifled the country's capacity for advancement. Its stock market remained near record lows for the better part of a decade. Real estate prices were similarly stuck in a slump.

Several economists have released hypotheses for why Japan's depression was so severe. Paul Krugman, a Distinguished Professor of Economics at the Graduate Center of the City of New York and a New York Times columnist, blames consumers for the length of Japan's financial crisis. In an effort to recover lost funds, many of Japan's average citizens "saved too much" and neglected to stimulate the economy's growth with regular spending practices. Aggregate demand all but disappeared, and the country fell into a deflationary spiral. In an article for the National Bureau of Economic Research, Charles Yuji Horioka similarly blames regular consumers for selfish spending habits. "The stagnation of investment," Horioka says, "especially private fixed investment, was the primary culprit" of the slowdown in Japan's economy. However, it's hard to fault individual spenders for their response to a disaster beyond their control. Household consumption slowed following "the stagnation of household disposable income, the decline in household wealth, and increased uncertainty about the future . . . " Other economists are less concerned with how the average Joe responded to the economic downturn and more interested in the country's unique age segmentation. Japan's aging demographic at the time demanded the economy perform unreasonably well to sustain its many retired citizens. The working class was incapable of supporting its elders. Still other financial experts place the blame squarely on the government's monetary policy.[14,15]

A balanced examination of Japan's mistakes will probably conclude that all the above factors and more played some role in prompting an economic collapse. But what bearing does the story of Japan's lost decade have on us?

Lessons Learned?

Economists identify several lessons to learn from Japan's lost decade.

1. Banks must act fast when a crisis begins. When the economy started to tank, the Bank of Japan was reluctant to intercede. Investors thus lost confidence which only worsened the problem.

2. Government spending doesn't always work. Japan hoped that contributions to projects that would benefit the public might spur on private spending and stimulate the dragging economy. The idea didn't work. Instead, the federal government found itself further in debt with an economy that showed little sign of improvement.

3. An aging demographic slows economic growth. The aging population in Japan posed a serious problem to the country's capacity for growth and any bounce-back. Raising the retirement age or increasing taxes may have, in theory, shortened the length of Japan's economic troubles.

4. Debt is a killer that keeps on killing. Even when Japan's economy showed signs of improvement, the country's massive debt stifled any hope of recovery for several years. Debt is what made the

---

[14] Charles Yuji Horioka. April 2006. The National Bureau of Economic Research. "The Causes of Japan's "Lost Decade": The Role of Household Consumption." https://www.nber.org/papers/w12142

[15] Justin Kuepper. September 18, 2019. The Balance. "What You Can Learn From Japan's Lost Decade." https://www.thebalance.com/japan-s-lost-decade-brief-history-and-lessons-1979056

recession so bad in the first place, and it prevented the drowning economy from coming up for air.

Lessons are all well and good, but they're only advantageous if we learn from them and make application. Unfortunately, the world seemed to forget many of Japan's mistakes as soon as the economy's condition improved. Still, United States policy makers learned something from Japan's example. According to billionaire investor and philanthropist Ray Dalio, it was from watching Japan that the accountable entities avoided a second American depression. But more could probably have been done to prevent what has become known as the Great American Recession.

America's Lost Decade

Most of you reading this book will remember the two major recessions that marked the first decade of America's twenty-first century (some economists consider them part of a single recessionary period). Your recollection may be colored with a number of emotions: shock, disappointment, anxiety, disbelief. You may have experienced tremendous loss. It wasn't all your fault, though. People in positions of great responsibility—including the federal government itself—allowed the United States economy to follow a pattern much like Japan's a decade earlier. It's of little surprise, then, that the end result was likewise similar to Japan's lost decade.

The 1990s were a monumental decade, not just for the United States, but the entire world. A little-known scientist named Tim Berners-Lee had invented what he called the "World Wide Web" in 1989. It was an information space that could be accessed by the internet, itself in its infant stages. *World Wide* Web was a bit of a misnomer, however. To access "the Web" required a web browser and none had been invented that achieved world-wide use. Berners-Lee himself had developed a web browser for his World Wide Web, but it failed to gain popularity.

Then, in 1993, a browser called Mosaic was released. Something about mosaic had universal appeal, an enigmatic quality which its predecessors lacked. The browser quickly became the de facto web browser and with it, Berners-Lee's World Wide Web lived up to its moniker. Internet service usage took off and household computer ownership became standard.

Within a couple years, tech-savvy entrepreneurs looked to capitalize on the internet's rising success. A new breed of business emerged; internet-only companies were the hottest new thing. I mean, what's a better business model than unprecedented access to consumers with hardly any overhead? Companies like Pets.com, eBay.com, and Amazon.com were received with incredible interest from consumers and investors alike. Anything with a ".com" suffix in the name was bound to succeed.

Many keen investors poured their money into "dot-com" stocks and experienced unparalleled growth. It was hard to invest in an internet company and *not* see immense returns. I remember stories of some investors who emptied their 401(k)s and other retirement accounts to invest in individual stocks within the internet business industry. Tying up all of your money in specific stock market assets is never a good idea, but who could blame them? Everyone was doing it and the lure of quick money could make even the most incorrigible miser salivate. Moreover, news and media outlets had nothing but good things to say about the internet investment trend.

It's normally a sign of quality and investor confidence when big banks start to get in on the action. By 1998, just about every major investment firm had a hot-ticket mutual fund that revolved around the internet. Finance experts everywhere hailed the value of these trendy investment vehicles. "E-commerce" became a household word. One article from 1998 talked about "excitement over the Internet space and e-business" among the world's top investors. Dot-com business and the mutual funds built around them were lauded as the only investments worth your money. An article entitled, "The Darlings of Tech Mutual Funds" made a compelling argument for the three highest grossing tech mutual funds—Munder NetNet, PIMCO Innovation Fund, and Dresdner RCM Global Technology Fund—citing their incomparable growth over just a few years and the "safety" they afforded investors. After all, these mutual funds were backed by some of the world's most accomplished and wealthy investment firms.[16]

Even highly respected and typically conservative finance journals like Forbes threw their lot in with the internet craze. An August 5, 1998 article enumerated the performance stats of several internet funds and emphasized how they had outperformed the S&P 500. They offered another benefit, responsible "hands-on management" for which there was "no comparison." How's that for inspiring investor confidence? Too bad they were selling seats on a sinking ship.[17]

For a while, tech stocks climbed without a ceiling in sight. But . . . what goes up must come down, and the stock market eventually came down in a big way. In early 2000, several mutual funds closed to new investors. The floor fell out from under them before the year's end.

Munder NetNet, one of the largest funds of the era, reported a 54 percent loss in value by the end of 2000. It's worth would continue to fall over the next several years until the mutual fund was dead entirely.

Many retirees found themselves, as the proverb goes, "up a creek without a paddle." If you'd invested all your money in the tech bubble, by 2002 your portfolio's value would have decreased by roughly 80 percent—quite a predicament for someone who plans to stop working. Unfortunately, that wasn't the last financial disaster to beset the 2000s.

---

[16] Dawn Kawamoto. July 30, 1998. CNET. "The Darlings of Tech Mutual Funds." https://www.cnet.com/news/the-darlings-of-tech-mutual-funds/
[17] Vicki Contavepsi. August 5, 1998. Forbes. "Forget Munder NetNet." https://www.forbes.com/1998/08/05/feat_side1.html#477e085042d1

Eight years later, just as the market seemed to have bounced back, another "bubble" developed: The housing bubble. It burst in 2008 when the Case-Shiller Home Price Index experienced its largest drop in history. The ensuing recession capped off a decade of generally dismal investment returns and finalized what would come to be known as The Great Recession, America's lost decade.

What Does It All Mean?

There are several major similarities between Japan's and the United States' lost decades, too many, in fact, to ignore. In both, stock market bubbles grew (and then popped) and real estate prices ballooned out of control, spurred on by unrealistic speculation. When each economy crashed, the countries' governing bodies responded with major bailouts that left the federal governments in extraordinary debt. There's one important difference between the two "lost decades," however: Japan's happened ten years earlier.

Japan's experience, and the development of its economy in the twenty-plus years since recovering from a significant economic depression, thus serve as a kind of financial almanac for the United States. Japan's modern financial history helps us predict how our own economy might adjust in coming years as we contend with massive national debt and the effects of recession. It affords us a unique perspective; we've seen how a country with an economy similar to the United States bounces back from a tremendous blow to its financial infrastructure. What do we learn?

First, the debt isn't going anywhere. As of this book's writing, the United States national debt sits just below $22 trillion. Japan, some twenty years removed from its recession, is still heavily in debt. It will take a long time for both governments to make any mentionable contribution to the repayment of their deficits. The national debt is shocking, but does it really matter for today's retiree?

In short, yes. It matters a great deal.

Japan has kept interest rates near all-time lows for two decades to minimize the interest expense on its national debt. The United States is following suit. For much of the American population, that's not such a bad thing. Low interest rates can be good. For retirees, however, it's a different story.

Low Interest Rates and the Retiree

Most of the time, the news and media suggest that low interest rates are to our benefit. That's because they cater to the working-age demographic. For retirees, however, or soon-to-be retirees, what's good for the working class can be detrimental to their retirement goals. That's a generalization but let me explain what I mean.

In the last chapter I discussed the three phases of financial life: Accumulation, preservation, distribution. A lot of the financial advice you hear in the news is directed toward investors in the accumulation phase: Young to middle-aged working people. That demographic is comprised of many borrowers. Young working people take out student loans to fund their educations, they take out loans to buy new cars, they get mortgages to buy new homes – all things for which consumers want low interest rates. But many retirees are passed that stage in their lives. They depend on interest rates to generate their income.

According to Brian Rehling, co-head of global fixed income at Wells Fargo Investment Institute, "the growing debt load and the aging demographics are disinflationary—it keeps rates low and it keeps inflation low." Low inflation sounds nice, but balance is important and right now things are at an extreme. "This low-rate environment is at the detriment of savers," Rehling continues. "People essentially have to save even more for retirement because those low rates and low returns mean that they're not going to have as much in retirement as they may have in a higher-rate environment."

Low rates of return are here to stay for the foreseeable future, Rehling says. "You have to come up with some creative solutions when the market is just not going to give you those higher returns that may have been commonplace in the past," he concludes.[18]

Basic stock market investment and high returns on traditional savings and retirement accounts aren't enough to fund a successful retirement these days. And they're not the only things missing from today's retirement landscape. Another "standard" retirement income source from decades past has fallen by the wayside: The trusty pension.

Pensions Aren't the Best Bet

The 1950s marked a turning point in the American economy and lifestyle. Much like the internet boom that would explode some forty years later, the 1950s experienced leaps and bounds in the world of technology. Among these new and improved technologies was the automobile. Sure, cars had been around for nearly a hundred years. But cars of the 1950s were unlike anything the world had ever seen.

A popular manufacturer of the day was Studebaker. It was founded in 1852 and, believe it or not, made its foray into automobile production with an electric car. Talk about ahead of the game. Studebaker made a good product and consumers loved it. There seemed to be no production capacity that could satisfy the voracious American appetite for glamorous new vehicles. At its peak, Studebaker employed about 23,000 people. Even by today's standards that's a respectable company.

---

[18] Scott Gamm. The Street. August 1, 2016. "How Government Debt Affects Your Retirement." https://www.thestreet.com/story/13658898/1/how-government-debt-affects-your-retirement.html

As was general practice in those days, each of the 23,000 workers was promised a pension. It was an excellent pension. Studebaker employees and retirees were among the highest paid in the automobile industry. In 1954, to patch up some financial mishaps, Studebaker was acquired by Packard, a more financially stable car maker. By 1956, to Packard's dismay, it was evident that Studebaker's financial "mishaps" were more like a series of train wrecks. By 1957, both companies had nearly succumbed to bankruptcy. Studebaker finally shut its doors in December 1963.

When Studebaker's production plant closed, the liability of the company's pension plan exceeded its assets by a whopping $15 million. At the time of this book's writing, that is worth $123 million! That's a lot of pensions that went unpaid.

For the first time ever, a major company failed to pay out the pensions it had promised its employees. Every employee between age forty and sixty, many of whom had devoted forty years of service to Studebaker, was granted just 15 percent of what his or her pension should have been. Employees under forty got nothing.

The story of Studebaker's rise and demise is important for two reasons. First, it illustrates the volatility of the financial world. It's another horrible truism, but financially speaking we must always *expect the unexpected*. The economy can crash, we can lose our jobs, we can incur surprise health expenses. Ultimately, our financial health is our own responsibility.

Second, Studebaker's failure was a defining moment in the development of the need for retirement planning. For many of us, especially if we are approaching retirement, we will remember our parents retiring with a pension. For them retirement planning was simple: do your work until you can collect your pension and Social Security kicks in. Easy as that. Personal savings was like gravy on top. Together, those three income sources were described as the three-legged stool of retirement. There was little to no stress and uncertainty involved. But Studebaker's financial faux pas set off a chain of events that complicated the retirement process.

The Studebaker disaster revealed a critical flaw in the pension system. Employers were under no legal obligation to fulfill the terms of their employees' pension plans. Shocking, right? But it's true. Sure, it's not like companies could just decide not to pay out. But if they went bankrupt, like Studebaker did, and happened to run out of money before they could fulfill their pension promises—oh well. There were zero repercussions and jilted Studebaker employees had no way to recover their tremendous losses.

To ensure that something like that would never happen again, Congress passed the Employee Retirement Income Security Act or ERISA. Employers would now be legally required to insure and protect their employees' pension funds. To accomplish this, the Pension Benefit Guaranty Corporation was established. It was fashioned after the organization that protects bank deposits, the Federal Deposit Insurance Corporation, or FDIC.

ERISA sounded good on paper and its inception was well intentioned. But, as you might imagine, big corporations didn't like the idea of setting money aside for future pensions that could be used in the moment to expand business. So, the law backfired. Rather than insure the pensions, companies decided simply to do away with pension plans altogether. Instead, the onus was transferred to the employee to fund his future retirement income.

Today, more than ever before, responsibility falls to retirees to ensure their financial futures. We cannot dictate the type of economy in which we'll retire. We can't guarantee that another recession won't come along during our retired years. We can't be sure that our employers will contribute much to our retirement nest egg. But we can plan for the worst so when the winds of economic change come our way, we'll be better prepared for the storm. This chapter has examined some retirement roadblocks that are beyond the retiree's control. But there are many risks that a well-prepared retiree can avoid with a little preparation. Chapter Four will evaluate a few major risks for today's retiring population.

Chapter Three Key Lessons:

• This is not your grandpa's retirement. The future is different than the past. Err on the side of caution and prepare for it.
• The economy will always go down again. You must plan to safeguard your retirement income regardless of external circumstances.
• You are responsible to ensure your own financial wellbeing.

Chapter Four

Risk in Retirement

I f you follow football—even casually like me—you might remember the Seahawks tremendous failure in 2014's Super Bowl XLIX. In case your recollection is a bit fuzzy, I'll give you the highlights.

With 26 seconds left on the clock, the Seahawks were losing by 4 points to the Patriots. But the game was theirs for the taking. It was second and goal—the endzone was one yard away—and the Seahawks had the best running back in the league: Marshawn "Beast Mode" Lynch. With three chances and one yard to go for a Super Bowl win, it would be hard for the Seahawks to lose.

And then they lost.

Russell Wilson, the Seahawk's beloved quarterback, opted to throw the ball. It's hard to say why. Maybe he thought it would fool the opposing team who were probably expecting the run. Maybe he reasoned that it minimized the chances of a fumble. Or maybe Wilson just wanted credit for the game winning throw. Whatever his thought process, the result was not what he'd hoped. Wilson's pass was intercepted by a Patriot's cornerback, Malcolm Butler, a rookie.

Do you remember that game? Seahawks fans are probably annoyed that I've made them relive the trauma. Here's what you might not remember, though: That was not the first time that a Seahawks team risked it all and failed in spectacular fashion. Nor was it the first time their quarterback was to blame.

The Seahawks were inaugurated into the NFL in 1973. The team got off to a slow start. By 2003, though, it seemed like the Seahawks were finally contenders for the Super Bowl. Their quarterback at the time, Matt Hasselback, was an average regular season player, but he thrived in the playoffs. To this day, Hasselback's playoff statistics rank in the top-20 among all quarterbacks in NFL history. Despite his resume, however, Matthew Hasselback is probably most well remembered for his conduct at the 2003 NFC divisional playoff game.

The Seahawks were playing the Green Bay Packers. After a bumpy first half, Hasselback bounced back in the second and forced the game into overtime. Hasselback had previously played for the Packers, but they'd traded him two years earlier. Maybe a chip on his shoulder drove him to play some of his best football. It may also have fueled his display of arrogance at the overtime coin toss.

Eager to beat his former team and fueled with competitive passion, Hasselback took the field along with his rival captain. The Seahawks won the coin toss. Hasselback made a point to declare his team's decision into the FOX sports microphone, "We want the ball, *and we're going to score.*"

His confidence shocked and inspired viewers around the country. Those were bold words from a quarterback who'd barely managed to force an overtime situation. Did he have what it'd take to back them up?

Nope.

After a few promising completions, Hasselback took the snap near the 50-yard line. He dropped back a quick five steps and threw a bullet to his left. The announcer erupted in hysterics— "intercepted by Al Harris! He has room! He could score! Nobody will catch him . . . and the Packers win!" It was a humiliating defeat for the Seahawks, and a humiliating moment for Matt Hasselback that would come to define his career in the NFL.

In both stories of the Seahawks' failures, what was key to the team's defeat? Overconfidence and inaccurate estimation of risk. In the final moments of two important games, the Seahawk's chose to risk it all and they misgauged the forces working against them. It's not that Russell Wilson and Matthew Hasselback were bad quarterbacks; but they took matters into their own hands and failed in execution.

Many soon-to-be retirees are likewise talented. I've met with hundreds of potential clients in my years as a financial advisor and most have been impressive people: CEOs, lawyers, entrepreneurs, master craftspeople. They're all bright and well-informed. But the most common problem I see among new clients is not understanding how much risk they're taking with their investments. High-risk, ill-advised investment decisions endanger their important retirement income. It's just not worth it.

The last few years before retirement (and the first few years *in* retirement when you're still figuring things out) are like the red zone in football. On a football field, the red zone is the last twenty yards before the endzone, where touchdowns are made. Good coaches know to change their team's play style when it enters the red zone because the stakes are higher and the repercussions of error increase. Russell Wilson and his Seahawks were deep in the red zone when he chose to make a risky call. It was an aggressive play and it backfired.

In Chapter Two, we outlined the phases of financial life. Once investors enter the preservation phase, they're in the figurative "red zone" of retirement. If you're reading this book, chances are that you're in the red zone. There's always risk in investment, but for aging investors things change a bit. The way you've interpreted risk throughout your career may not apply to your current circumstances. It's important to redefine risk through the lens of retirement planning.

Drawdown Risk

When soon-to-be retirees think of financial risk, sometimes they oversimplify the equation. Some new clients have told me that in their evaluation of risk, they make sure to keep a steady ratio of stocks to bonds. If stocks start to make up too much of their portfolio, they adjust to minimize risk. They're not necessarily wrong. Too much exposure to stock market volatility is a primary risk for investors, but that's true for all investors. Aging investors, however, need to reevaluate their tolerance for risk with retirement in mind.

I've heard it said that for every three dollars invested in bonds, it's safe to invest one dollar in stocks. Bonds aren't a great investment option for everyone these days, but we'll address that subject later on. The point is conventional wisdom might have us invest about 25 percent of our money in the stock market and put the rest in more conservative investment vehicles. Is that a wise course of action for people nearing retirement?

When I was in the midst of my studies for the RICP designation, one of my professors said, "the definition of risk changes at the point of retirement." The idea harkens back to the phases of financial life. To a young investor in the accumulation phase of life, risk means simply "the probability of loss." As we shift into the preservation and distribution phases, risk also starts to mean "the probability that I'll run out of money in retirement." That subtle adjustment in mindset can make a world of difference in our evaluation of risk.

I have many potential clients come to my office confident they already have a solid and "safe" plan for retirement. Recently, a couple in their early sixties came into my office. Let's call them Rob and Gillian Gershom. They had attended one of my workshops some months earlier and decided later to schedule an appointment.

Rob made it clear from the start, they were only there for a second opinion. They were not in need of my financial services, he said. In fact, they didn't really want me to *do* anything at all. The Gershoms had a comprehensive investment portfolio, it was well-diversified, and their retirement was all set. Unsurprisingly, I found out later that it was Gillian who had convinced her husband to pay me a visit.

Rob's request wasn't that unusual, and I was happy to sit down with the Gershoms and evaluate the quality of their current plans for retirement. Their "plan" had been pieced together by the Gershoms' broker, a friend of theirs with whom they'd worked for years. Just from a quick look-through of their portfolio, I suspected that this plan hadn't changed much in the many years since Rob and Gillian first compiled it. But the Gershoms were now within five years of retirement. They were probably unaware of the risk inherent to their investment style. Not that they didn't understand stock market risk, but they probably didn't understand how it augments for people at their station in life.

After taking a few more minutes to review the Gershoms' assets, I asked them to estimate their comfortable risk tolerance. It's something I ask all the families we serve. "With plans to retire in the next few years," I said, "how much of all this stuff are you potentially willing to subject to loss?"

Rob laughed. "None of it," he said.

I laughed too. "Of course, no one is quite *willing* to give up money," I responded. "But with many of your assets invested in mutual funds, 401(k)s, stocks, etcetera, there will always be the chance that you lose some money when the market drops. So, assuming everything goes south, what is the absolute limit that you could stand to give up? What percentage of everything you have could you subject to drawdown risk and still be all right?"

Rob and Gillian looked at each other and thought for a minute. Then Rob spoke up, "I'd say about 15 percent."

Let me tell you, 10 to 15 percent is almost always the number people tell me. It may not sound like a lot, but some people don't seem to realize that 15 percent of a million dollars is $150,000. When we assign real dollars and cents to 15 percent, it's often more than people are genuinely willing to subject to potential loss. I didn't say that to Rob and Gillian, though, at least not right away. Instead, we scheduled a second meeting in a couple weeks so that my team and I could examine the Gershoms' financial records and evaluate exactly how much risk they carried.

Two weeks later I sat down with the Gershoms for the second time to tell them what I'd discovered. Can you guess how much they stood to lose from their portfolio in the event of a sharp market downturn? It wasn't 15 percent.

Rob and Gillian were in a position to lose nearly 37 percent: More than double what they estimated they could afford. In reality, 15 percent was probably already a dangerously high figure. But 37 percent loss in retirement would almost certainly force the Gershoms back into the working world. With retirement right around the corner, Rob and Gillian were positioned for trouble if the stock market tanked like it did in 2008. As you can imagine, they were horrified at that revelation, and they were eager to enact a plan to de-risk their portfolio.

Experiences like that are upsetting to me. The Gershoms were good people, and they were taking steps to ensure they could retire with confidence. So, it wasn't with the Gershoms that I have a problem. What upsets me is Rob and Gillian's broker led them to believe that their portfolio was bulletproof when that couldn't have been further from the truth. My grandpa used to tell me, "never invest money you can't afford to lose." In his day, that made sense. He could survive on his savings and pension alone. Any extra money, he'd invest without a care in the world. Sure, he didn't want to lose it. But if the market tanked and his invested money was gone, it wasn't the end of the world. That cannot be said of investment today. Unfortunately, for most of us, we *need* to invest money that we will someday need, otherwise there's no way to meet our basic retirement goals. For the twenty-first century retiree, then, it's better to say, "never invest money that you need in the *short-term*." That's what the Gershoms' portfolio needed to reflect. They couldn't avoid risk altogether, but neither could they stand to invest according to my grandfather's outmoded philosophy.

The amount investors stand to lose is called *maximum drawdown*. One of my primary goals as a financial advisor is to help clients reduce maximum drawdown as much as possible without sacrificing healthy growth. Almost every prospective family I've met has unknowingly carried an inappropriate maximum drawdown for their circumstances. By means of a portfolio stress test and programs like Morningstar, an investment research tool, it's straightforward to evaluate how much risk investors have and even how long it could take to recover from the effects of stock market crashes. And believe me, market crashes will come again. Markets operate in cycles and crashes are just a regular part of the cycle. They're normal. That's part of why it's so important to plan for market crashes; you can be sure they'll always happen again.

If the Gershoms had lost 37 percent of their portfolio, especially at the start of their retirement, it could have taken five to eight years for them to recover their losses, assuming they went back to work. If, hypothetically, they sustained a nearly 40 percent loss and decided to *stay* retired, Rob and Gillian might have run out of money in the course of their retired life. That's largely due to a second financial construct: The sequence of returns.

Sequence of Returns Risk

Before I explain the sequence of returns, it's important to understand the concept of standard deviation. Standard deviation is the dispersion, or spread, of a dataset from its average. The more dispersed your data, the higher the standard deviation. In a financial context, standard deviation measures the volatility of an investment based on historical divergence from its average return. The higher an investment's standard deviation, the less confident we are in its consistency of return. Consistency is everything for the retired investor. It doesn't matter if on average your portfolio grows 12 percent if for three years it's experiencing negative returns when you are withdrawing income to cover your needs. Those three years, for the retired investor, may be enough to derail retirement expectations because of what we call the "sequence of returns."

To illustrate the sequence of returns, imagine that you have $10 to invest in a fictional account that gives daily returns. Every day after your investment, you will need to withdraw $1 to provide for daily expenses. Your $10 is invested entirely in stock market options and the daily return is out of your control.

On your first day, you experience a staggering 50 percent return! Now you have $15 before withdrawing $1. At day's end, your account shows $14. On day two, you again see 50 percent growth. That brings your account balance, after withdrawing a second dollar, to $20. On day three, things turn for the worse. Our hypothetical market crashes and you lose 50 percent. Now you have $9 at the end of the day. But it gets worse. Day four experiences another 50 percent drop in value which brings your balance to $3.50. You're down from your initial investment, but if the market improves there's a good chance you'll recover.

Now let's imagine that your account experiences the same two days of 50 percent growth and two days of 50 percent loss, but in reverse order. In other words, let's change the *sequence* of your returns. Now, the original $10—after two days of loss and with daily withdrawals of $1—is reduced to $1. At that point, it doesn't matter that the market sees 50 percent growth in the next two days. At the end of day three you'll have $0.50. At the end of day four your account is in the negative. That's how powerful the sequence of returns can be.

You're probably sick of math at this point, but can you see why the sequence of returns matters so much more to retirees? It's because they *have* to withdraw money regardless of what the market is doing.

That leaves their accounts with much less earning capacity if there's a time of sustained loss. In our example, if we remove the daily withdrawals, sequence is rendered irrelevant. In both situations the final balance would come to $5.65.

You've probably heard it said that investors earn on average about 8 percent return on stock market investments per year. That's not to say that every year the stock market sees eight percent growth. Rather, eight percent is the *annualized* rate of return taken over many years of data. In reality, the stock market can fluctuate dramatically in its performance from year to year. The order in which it experiences years of growth or loss can make or break a retiree's portfolio if it depends too heavily on stock market trends. (Now I use 8 percent as an example only; depending on what you're invested in, 8 percent may be entirely too high, but we use it for illustrative reasons here only.)

The following tables compare two hypothetical retirees, James and Claire, with assets invested mostly in the stock market. They each experience an 8.03 percent annualized rate of return, but as you'll see, it doesn't matter. James and Claire end up with very different final balances because they experience different sequence of returns.

When James retires, the market is down and his first three years see only losses. Meanwhile, James is withdrawing necessary retirement income. When things finally improve, James' account has been crippled. Even with many years of positive return, his balance steadily falls until he runs out of money eighteen years into retirement.

Claire retires with the same original nest egg, but she is fortunate enough to retire when the market is soaring. Eventually she experiences years of loss just like James did, but it doesn't matter. Her balance has had time to grow. After twenty-four years, Claire is more than three times wealthier than when she retired. What made such a difference for Claire? It's not that she invested more wisely than James, nor that she had more money from the outset. The only difference was her sequence of returns.

As you've probably discerned by now, the sequence of returns is out of investors' control if their money is subject to stock market instability. The key, then, to minimizing sequence of return risk is to minimize stock market exposure and look for investment vehicles that have low standard deviation. Remember, standard deviation measures the variability of return from year to year. Sequence of return risk is a direct consequence of investments with high standard deviation.

The following example is hypothetical and does not represent any specific investment and does not take into account taxes or investment fees.

Age	Market	Withdrawal	Nest egg
		James	
64			**$500,000**
65	-10.14%	$25,000	$500,000
66	-13.04%	$25,750	$426,839
67	-23.37%	$26,523	$348,776
68	14.62%	$27,318	$246,956
69	2.03%	$28,138	$251,750
70	12.40%	$28,982	$228,146
71	27.25%	$29,851	$223,862
72	-6.65%	$30,747	$246,879
73	26.31%	$31,669	$201,956
74	4.46%	$32,619	$215,084
75	7.06%	$33,598	$190,610
76	-1.54%	$34,606	$168,090
77	34.11%	$35,644	$131,429
78	20.26%	$36,713	$128,458
79	31.01%	$37,815	$110,335
80	26.67%	$38,949	$95,008
81	19.53%	$40,118	$71,009
82	26.38%	$36,923	$36,923
83	-38.49%	$0	$0
84	3.00%		
85	13.62%		
86	3.53%		
87	26.38%		
88	23.45%		
89	12.78%		

Average Return	Total Withdrawal
8.03%	$580,963

Claire			
Age	Market	Withdrawal	Nest egg
64			**$500,000**
65	12.78%	$25,000	$500,000
66	23.45%	$25,750	$535,716
67	26.38%	$26,523	$629,575
68	3.53%	$27,318	$762,140
69	13.62%	$28,138	$760,755
70	3.00%	$28,982	$832,396
71	-38.49%	$29,851	$827,524
72	26.38%	$30,747	$490,684
73	19.53%	$31,669	$581,270
74	26.67%	$32,619	$656,916
75	31.10%	$33,598	$790,788
76	20.26%	$34,606	$991,981
77	34.11%	$35,644	$1,151,375
78	-1.54%	$36,713	$1,496,314
79	7.06%	$37,815	$1,437,133
80	4.46%	$38,949	$1,498,042
81	26.31%	$40,118	$1,524,231
82	-6.56%	$41,321	$1,874,535
83	27.25%	$42,561	$1,712,970
84	12.40%	$43,838	$2,125,604
85	2.03%	$45,153	$2,339,923
86	14.37%	$46,507	$2,341,297
87	-23.27%	$47,903	$2,630,297
88	-13.04%	$49,340	$1,978,993
89	-10.14%	$50,820	$1,677,975

Average Return	**Total Withdrawal**
8.03%	$911,482

The following tables compare two portfolios. Each has a 6.91 percent average return but different standard deviations. The data looks similar to our previous comparison, but notice the included standard deviations. Clearly, high standard deviation adds more risk to a portfolio when a person is relying on this portfolio for income.

Taking Income: Portfolio 1

Year	Return	Start of Year Value	Earnings	Withdrawal
2000	-9.06%	$1,000,000	-$90,600	-$50,000
2001	-12.02%	$859,400	-$103,300	-$50,000
2002	-22.15%	$706,100	-$156,401	-$50,000
2003	28.50%	$499,699	$142,414	-$50,000
2004	10.74%	$592,113	$63,593	-$50,000
2005	4.77%	$605,706	$28,892	-$50,000
2006	15.64%	$584,598	$91,431	-$50,000
2007	5.39%	$626,029	$33,743	-$50,000
2008	-37.02%	$609,772	-$225,738	-$50,000
2009	26.49%	$334,035	$88,486	-$50,000
2010	14.91%	$372,520	$55,543	-$50,000
2011	1.97%	$378,063	$7,448	-$50,000
2012	15.82%	$335,511	$53,078	-$50,000
2013	32.18%	$338,589	$108,958	-$50,000
2014	13.51%	$397,547	$53,709	-$50,000
2015	1.25%	$401,255	$5,016	-$50,000
2016	11.82%	$356,271	$42,111	-$50,000
2017	21.67%	$348,382	$75,494	-$50,000
		$373,877		
Average	6.91%			
Standard Deviation	17.92%			

The above table is intended to illustrate the results of a hypothetical investment of $1 million in the Vanguard 500 Index beginning on the first trading day of 2000 and held through the last trading day of 2017, with $50,000 withdrawn from the investment on an annual basis. It is assumed that any dividends and other earnings are reinvested an no allowances for external advisory fees have been made. The results may vary significantly if the beginning day and/or the ending day is altered. The holdings comprising the fund have changed over time and are likely to change in the future. The fund performance and other information was acquired from Morningstar Direct. It is believed to be accurate but has not been independently verified by Brindle & Bay Advisors Group, LLC. Past performance is not necessarily indicative of future results. Investment advisory services offered through Brindle & Bay Wealth Management LLC, a Registered Investment Advisor.

Taking Income: Portfolio 2

Year	Return	Start of Year Balance	Earnings	Withdrawal
2000	8.15%	$1,000,000	$81,500	-$50,000
2001	-2.44%	$1,031,500	-$25,169	-$50,000
2002	0.34%	$956,331	$3,252	-$50,000
2003	19.98%	$909,583	$181,735	-$50,000
2004	12.10%	$1,041,318	$125,999	-$50,000
2005	9.73%	$1,117,317	$108,715	-$50,000
2006	11.38%	$1,176,032	$133,832	-$50,000
2007	7.64%	$1,259,864	$96,254	-$50,000
2008	-4.12%	$1,306,118	-$53,812	-$50,000
2009	5.19%	$1,202,306	$62,400	-$50,000
2010	12.11%	$1,214,706	$147,101	-$50,000
2011	11.09%	$1,311,807	$145,479	-$50,000
2012	8.04%	$1,407,286	$113,146	-$50,000
2013	0.11%	$1,470,432	$1,617	-$50,000
2014	13.15%	$1,422,049	$186,999	-$50,000
2015	-5.08%	$1,559,049	-$79,200	-$50,000
2016	4.86%	$1,429,849	$69,491	-$50,000
2017	12.24%	$1,449,340	$177,399	-$50,000
		$1,576,739		
Average	6.91%			
Standard Deviation	6.82%			

The above table is intended to illustrate the potential results of a hypothetical investment of $1 million with $50,000 withdrawn from the investment on an annual basis in a typical mix of securities that would yield a series of returns less volatile than the returns of an investment that intends to track the S&P 500® over the same time period, beginning on the first trading day of 2000 and held through the last trading day of 2017. The table does not represent the results of an investment of an actual security or mix of securities. Investment advisory services offered through Brindle & Bay Wealth Management, LLC, a Registered Investment Advisor. Investing involves risk, including the potential loss of principal.

Neither portfolio experienced unreasonable annualized return. But with savvy investments and a degree of independence from the stock market, the second portfolio saw over 50 percent growth in 18 years. You can use strategies to help reduce the standard deviation of your portfolio without sacrificing return potential. The goal of de-risking and reducing standard deviation is to remove some money from risk and *also* to get a return. The types of places to put money might include bank CDs, Treasury bonds, fixed annuities, and fixed indexed annuities. In later chapters, we'll discuss some of these options in greater detail. But first, it's important to understand how retirees should view their retirement planning process. A strong low-risk portfolio is only a first step. But retirees need to know exactly how they'll withdraw money to fund their retirement income. For that, retirees must understand what systems they do—or don't—have in place.

Chapter Four Key Lessons:

• Risk in your portfolio can be evaluated by observing your average return in relation to its standard deviation. Ask your advisor for a portfolio stress test. This should include a long-term average, long term standard deviation and the maximum drawdown.

• A sound plan should have a method of reducing sequence of returns risk, possibly something that does not allocate all money in the stock market while also aiming for modest returns elsewhere.

Chapter Five
Systems

I f you assembled a group of the smartest people on earth, endowed them with tens of billions of dollars, and told them to invest it, what investment strategy do you think they would employ? Would they look for undervalued initial public offerings, opportunities in venture capitalism, or maybe to invest in foreign emerging economies? All those options promise huge potential returns on investment. They also carry the risk of tremendous loss. Maybe our hypothetical think tank would choose to go a more traditionally conservative route and invest in government bonds and certificates of deposit. Not a bad idea, but in today's economy with historically low interest rates, the sacrifice on return may be too much to justify the added protection.

Fortunately, we don't have to guess how a group of the smartest people in the world would invest billions of dollars. Such groups exist. The world's top universities have billions of dollars in their investment portfolios and they employ many of the world's smartest people to manage their investment accounts. How are places like Harvard, Stanford, and Yale investing their money?

Simon Moore is a financial expert and the Chief Financial Officer of the investment app Moola. You know a guy is good with money when he handles an *investment* company's investments. (No guarantees here, he doesn't have a crystal ball to promise investment success, but he is a pretty smart guy). He's also been the CIO at FutureAdvisor and is the author of a successful book on automated investing. He suggests that the university model of investment is how retirees should look to develop their portfolios. "Similar to many of us," Moore says, "universities are essentially looking for a healthy long-term return on their money with some degree of stability." It's not the way young working people typically invest. If your goals are short term, like to save enough for "a deposit on a home in two years," you may want to look elsewhere for an investment model, Moore says. But, he continues, "if you have long term savings objectives such as saving for retirement in a few decades, then there's a lot to be learned from what places like Harvard are doing with their money." So, what are Ivy League colleges doing that retirees should imitate?[19]

Universities invest in a variety of things. They take diversification to heart and allocate their resources over a number of asset classes to help ensure a measure of stability. Different universities may choose different investment avenues, but there's one important constant: "universities are looking to pay themselves an income from their endowment." Sound familiar? That's exactly the goal of retirees. So how do universities guarantee the income they need and seek consistent returns even through market ups and downs? They use systems.

What's A System?

At my workshops, I often meet soon-to-be retirees who have been accomplished investors throughout their working years. Many have developed respectable retirement nest eggs. They have sophisticated

---

[19] Simon Moore. Forbes. June 13, 2017. "What You Can Learn from Harvard's, Stanford's and Yale's Investments."
https://www.forbes.com/sites/simonmoore/2017/06/13/what-you-can-learn-from-harvards-stanfords-and-yales-investments/#628e5cd11a3d

portfolios, but what comes next? How do they start *using* their portfolio? That seemingly basic question stumps many smart investors. People want to know how to spend the money they've saved, but the answer to that question can be elusive. Investors attend workshops, read articles, confer with friends, and it seems like every resource gives a different method. It seems like many of them would work. If you've felt that way, don't worry. You're right. There are many withdrawal strategies and several of them are effective.

When I was working toward a professional designation from The American College of Financial Services, I learned from a professor named Jamie Hopkins. He was the head grader of my capstone project for a financial designation I was working on. Jamie was a distinguished economist and frequent contributor to finance journals like Forbes. I approached Jamie one day with a proposal for a system of retirement income planning. I wanted his feedback because in a world full of income strategies, how could I be sure that one was superior to any other? Jamie thought for a second and said, "Nick, there are a million ways that people do income planning. Most of them work. The main thing is that you don't put somebody at too much risk."

In the time since that encounter with Professor Hopkins, I can say from my own experience that he was absolutely right. Many strategies, or systems, work. What's important, is that within the system you choose, your financial advisor takes great care to help you minimize risk. You want to avoid pulling money from a "squiggly line account," that is, one in which the rate of return fluctuates frequently whenever possible. That leaves two buckets, really. One from which income is withdrawn, often an annuity withdrawal, pension income, or Social Security, and another designed exclusively for growth potential. With that in mind, there are a few basic system types many retired investors employ to generate decades of stable income. I'll give a brief overview of a few. While each system can work well, they won't all be a good choice for *you*. My intention here is to familiarize you with your options, not to give blanket advice. Your portfolio will likely lend itself better to some systems than others. Determining your best course of action is best handled in person with a trusted financial advisor.

A System Only Works if You Use It

Before I jump into descriptions of some well-known systems, I have to address this point. After reading the subheading you probably thought, "um yeah obviously . . . " But give me a chance to explain.

I have a client whom we'll call Tom. You've heard the expression, "don't judge a book by its cover?" Well, Tom is the embodiment of that adage. Nothing about his kind personality is evidenced by his (stereotypically) terrifying appearance. Tom is a large, burly man. He's a lifelong Harley Davidson biker and he looks like it.

A few years ago, I walked into the office and found Tom sitting in my waiting room in his customary uniform: An aged Harley cut-off t-shirt and chrome-featured leather vest that steered clear of his muscular tattooed arms. I'd only met with Tom a few times by this point, so I was still startled when I saw him on my couch.

Tom was already retired. We'd reworked his portfolio to dispense with needless risk and set him up with a withdrawal system. But Tom had come into my office that morning to ask if he could withdraw a little extra to pay for some new chrome Harley pipes and new riding gear. He was pretty sure he shouldn't withdraw extra cash, so he planned to make some extra cash driving for Uber.

I was stunned. Drive for Uber? Why in the world would Tom, a retired man who'd worked hard his entire life, *drive for Uber*? We had a system in place that would allow for him to withdraw extra here and there for spending needs. But then it struck me, Tom *knew* he had a plan that worked well and provided him with regular income, but he failed to recognize that a system is all-inclusive. Every aspect of life that involves money should be accounted for in a competent system.

Tom thought his system of withdrawal was just an automated way to get his monthly check. But a system does so much more.

There was a second problem in Tom's understanding, however. When Tom came to my office that day, the stock market had just reported negative returns for the fifth day in a row in a market that was down all year. Tom was panicking. He was the kind of guy that watched financial news every day. Now, his emotions were getting the best of him. But here's the thing: Tom's portfolio was all set up properly for him, but he just needed help with his perspective. We reviewed his plan and instead of reacting to the low market and reducing his income, the system allowed Tom to maintain his standard of living without sacrificing valuable assets or shortening the longevity of his retirement portfolio. Tom was still thinking like a stock market investor, but we'd worked out a plan that accounted for market volatility. He just hadn't familiarized himself with how the system worked.

Here's my point: a system only works well if you *understand* it and *trust* it. Tom simply had to settle into retired life and get more familiar with his plan.

Fortunately, Tom stuck it out and allowed his system to do its job. He was stressing for no reason. That's the beauty of a carefully managed system. They allow us to make decisions in advance so that when unforeseen circumstances arise, we aren't forced to react emotionally or to make difficult decisions.

Income Floor Systems

Let's first examine one of the most basic withdrawal systems, the income floor system. Also called "expense-matching," an income floor system is comprised of what may be described as two distinct portfolios types. To account for essential expenses, income floor plans establish a portfolio of low-risk investment vehicles from which necessary income can be withdrawn. It might include things like annuities, government bonds, certificates of deposit, or treasuries. Any discretionary expenses, the "wants" instead of "needs" are paid for by means of more aggressive investment types that are subject to higher risk. Money from the first portfolio is the income floor is reliable and serves as the minimum figure you can expect from month to month. However, most of the time you can expect to make more when you include your riskier assets. Even in times of market downturn, though, there's no need to worry. You may not have the funds to buy that new jet ski that you've had your eye on, but your vital expenses should always be covered.

The income floor system is beautiful in its simplicity. It's hard to mess up. Once you've established the system of achieving your minimum necessary income, you can leave those investments alone and just collect your check. If you're itching to tinker with something, you can make adjustments to the second half of your system, the part that pays for discretionary funds. Even if things turn for the worse, you'll never make less than what you need (assuming your needs haven't risen significantly since you made your plan).

There is one major disadvantage that I see to the income floor method. Some people end up with not much left to contribute to their discretionary funds. A significant portion of your portfolio will have to go toward funding the "floor" because fixed products tend to have low returns. If that doesn't bother you and these conservative options appeal to you, then the income floor method may be a good option for you. A word of caution, though: If the portfolio is not managed carefully, it may fail to grow commensurate with the inflation rate, which then devalues your money.

The Bucket Approach

Bucketing is similar to the income floor method in the way it balances low-risk and high-risk investment options. Money is allocated to different "buckets" which each represent segments of time. For example, an investor may use a three-bucket strategy. In bucket number one, the investor puts enough money to pay for the first five years of retirement. That money is invested in lower risk options like treasuries. One can't expect much growth from that bucket, but it's essentially guaranteed.

Bucket two might be for years six through ten of retirement. Those funds are invested in mid-term, moderate investments that offer the potential for higher rates of return at the expense of some extra risk.

Finally, bucket three covers everything after the first ten years of retirement. When the investor retires, money in bucket three is sometimes invested in more aggressive high-risk, high-return potential investment vehicles. The level of risk may be adjusted as the investor approaches the time during which he or she needs to withdraw from bucket three.

The bucket approach can be organized in several ways. It may include more than three buckets, but the principle is always the same. Each bucket contains assets of increasing risk and higher return potential that corresponds to different segments of time that cover the duration of retirement.

Bucketing sounds good in theory, but I think it's overcomplicated. Studies have shown there is no mathematical advantage to a bucket system than using "one bucket" with a systematic withdrawal (which I'll explain next).[20] That's not to say that bucket systems are valueless,

---

[20] Robert Laura. *Forbes*. February 21, 2015. "Does the Retirement Buckets Strategy Really Work?"; Rebecca Lake *U.S. News & World Report*. November 10, 2017. "The Pros and Cons of a Bucket Savings Strategy." https://money.usnews.com/investing/investing-101/articles/2017-11-10/the-pros-and-cons-of-a-bucket-savings-strategy

however. The primary benefit is psychological. Many retired investors take solace in knowing, as they progress through retirement, the next few years are planned for with risk-appropriate options. It's not uncommon for retirees to deviate from their withdrawal strategy if they aren't confident that it will provide what they need, even when that strategy is more than capable of delivering sustainable income. For that reason, the bucket approach can be a way to help alleviate retiree stress.

Systematic Withdrawals

Remember in Chapter Two when I talked about the 4 percent rule? Systematic withdrawal is the next evolution in that system. "But wait," you might be thinking, "I thought you said that the 4 percent rule had many failings?" Yes, the 4 percent rule didn't work as universally as its inventor, William Bengen, would have hoped. But his idea wasn't entirely fallacious. In theory, the 4 percent rule has much merit, but it's often considered too safe for some and too aggressive for others. Its functionality depends on how your portfolio is managed, how many equities are involved, the current market environment, and your age at retirement. With some tweaking, though, the four percent rule can become a reliable retirement strategy. Finance experts call the new and improved version, "systematic withdrawal strategy."

The basic premise of systematic withdrawals is to determine a safe fixed withdrawal percentage for the retiree, but reevaluate and rebalance the investment portfolio often to determine whether that percentage ought to change slightly. As you can imagine, this system requires more contact with your financial advisor than in the previous systems. You and your advisor will have to monitor your spending each year and adjust to account for investment returns to help ensure your portfolio never runs dry. Perhaps more than with any other system I've mentioned so far, a systematic withdrawal strategy requires an excellent financial advisor whom you trust implicitly.

Keep in mind this derivative of the 4 percent rule has a big downside. It can sometimes fail to produce enough income. To guarantee the longevity of your portfolio, some years may call for a withdrawal far short of four percent. Often, that won't be enough. Fortunately, there's usually an alternative system for your needs that isn't based on systematic withdrawals.

Dynamic Withdrawal

Every system has certain pros and cons. What if we combined the benefits of many systems together while attempting to minimize the shortcomings? Finance experts and economists tussled with that question for a long time and believe that they have devised a solution called "dynamic withdrawal strategy" or "ratcheting withdrawal strategy." In my office, we employ special software to put this system into action.

Most retirees want to spend more money while they're young and capable and wouldn't mind cutting back some as they age. They also want confidence that they won't run out of money during their retired years. In a perfect world, the 4 percent rule would provide income over several decades, but it still wouldn't provide enough for what most retirees hope to do with their newfound freedom. Retirees could just throw caution to the wind and withdraw as much as they want in the hope that a strong market will sustain their reckless spending, but there's little chance that would work in practice. But what if retirees could plan for more: More money when they want it with a level of assurance from a strong financial plan? Well, nothing can ever be perfect, and we can't make guarantees, but the dynamic withdrawals system attempts to offer a better solution.

A dynamic withdrawal strategy operates on an up-to-date software simulation. Instead of a fixed amount for life, the family makes an annual decision on their withdrawal amount. They then set the income on auto pilot for the year. This allows them to remain involved and stay flexible, yet it keeps things simple. Unlike the 4 percent rule for life, they might be withdrawing 8 percent for a few years of retirement because they will actually reduce down to 3 percent or even less later. This allows for the family to spend more now and less later with a level of confidence. Each year the plan is updated and the outcome of the simulation guides any needed adjustments. Some people seem to prefer this plan as they are paying off RVs, taking more vacations, and enjoying their retirement.

I don't recommend enacting a system of dynamic withdrawals without professional assistance. There are important nuances that a trained advisor will understand that are critical to your portfolio's health and performance. Because this type of planning requires an ongoing relationship with an advisory team rather than a self-service approach, it is a little rarer.

Get the Most Out of Your Retirement

With any system, the point is to make the best retirement possible. We want low stress, longevity, and maximum income. There are different ways to accomplish that objective, but in my experience, a dynamic withdrawal strategy, guided by an advisory team, is a powerful way to plan for retirement.

My client Tom, whom I mentioned earlier, used a dynamic withdrawal system to plan his retirement. Tom was an emotional investor. He needed the structure and rules of a system to prevent him from making rash decisions. Maybe you're not sold on the idea of withdrawal systems, though. That's all right, you might just be like a friend of Tom's named Al.

Al was also a biker. Like Tom, Al liked to wear cut-off Harley shirts and leather vests and his arms were also covered in tattoos. But Al daylighted as a courtroom attorney, clad in stifling suits and ties. Al's day job came with an impressive salary, and by the time he was ready to retire, his retirement nest egg was impressive to say the least.

Tom and Al and their wives liked to hang out at a local spin class (that's right, four bikers congregating at a spin class). One morning before class, Tom told Al about his retirement plans and the dynamic withdrawal strategy he was using to manage his withdrawals. That all sounded well and good, Al said, but he preferred to keep things simple. Al would withdraw a simple 3.5 percent per year. He wanted to play it safe and never run out of money.

Al was a wealthy man. Three and a half percent of his portfolio was probably enough to live on, and he valued the simplicity and security of his basic withdrawal plan. But was it *really* the most he could afford to withdraw? Al was smart, but I believe that he sacrificed some standard of living just to avoid learning a retirement system.

You can choose to follow a basic method of withdrawal like Al and if your portfolio is large enough, you'll probably make it through retirement without issue. But with a well-thought-out system, you could potentially improve the quality of your retirement years without sacrificing confidence in your nest egg's security. It may take some extra planning, but the years of added income could make it worth your time and effort.

Chapter Five Key Lessons

• There are many methods that can be used to create an income plan. One important thing to remember is to not have too much risk. Another important consideration is to avoid pulling your money from a "squiggly line account."

• Systems allow us to put things on autopilot. They can give us reassurance that an action is going to happen again and again.

• You can withdraw a straight percentage, or you can adjust withdrawals based on your goals. You might be able to spend more in the early years of retirement if you are willing to spend less later.

Chapter Six
Annuities – Are They Worth It?

W hat's the deal with annuities? The words "annuity" and "annuitize" have been thrown around in the financial and retirement planning communities for over thirty years. Still, many don't understand how annuities work or whether an annuity will make a valuable contribution to their retirement portfolios. This chapter, I hope, sets the record straight.

Now just to be clear, this is not an endorsement of any product, nor do I posit that annuities should be in *every* retiree's income plan. In fact, as you'll see later, there are some annuities I think retirees should avoid like the plague. Personal circumstance is one of the greatest determining factors in the purchase of any financial product, and annuities are no exception. What's good for one retiree may not work for another. Conversely, a product that puts one investor's assets at inordinate risk can work wonders in a different portfolio.

Do not purchase an annuity without a thorough evaluation of your personal circumstances.

I cannot emphasize this point enough. You may encounter "financial advisors" who are little more than glorified annuity salesman. They might not be your best source for financial advice. Annuities should at most constitute a piece in your larger retirement plan. No matter what anyone tells you, *annuities are not an income plan* unto themselves.

A Bit of History

Although annuities have been popularized within the last thirty years, they have existed in concept for millennia.

The word "annuity" comes from the Latin, "annua," which means "yearly stipend." (The word "annual" is also derived from annua.) When the Caesars reigned, annua represented a formal contract that guaranteed payments after an individual contributed a single lump sum. Payments would continue until the individual's death or a previously agreed upon time.

A gentleman named Gnaeus Domitius Annuis Ulpianis was one of the first to deal a contractual annuity. Whether the word is derived from his third name is unconfirmed. The most common annuitants in ancient Rome were soldiers who were given annuities as part of their military compensation; a retirement plan of sorts. (By the way, if you haven't visited Rome, I highly recommend touring the Vatican and the Roman Colosseum. Ol' Gnaeus would have walked those same streets about 2,000 years ago.)

The same trend continued in the middle ages with feudal lords and kings using the lump sum contributions from annuities to fund their constant wars. I imagine they hoped that soldiers would die before having the opportunity to cash in on the promised lifetime wages. In any case, the annuity concept was taking off and it would continue to evolve in Europe into the modern era.

In 1759, the annuity made its way to the American colonies. Annuities were not the primary retirement package of the military, however, but rather the church. Annuities were funded by church patrons and used to support pastors and their families. Eventually, annuity contracts were opened up to more than just ministers. Even

Benjamin Franklin famously invested in annuities, eventually leaving some to the cities of Boston and Philadelphia in his will.[21]

So How Does It Work *Today*?

Annuities, at least in their very essence, have not changed much since ancient Rome. But today, annuities live under the umbrella of the insurance industry.

People buy insurance for many reasons. There's car insurance to protect drivers' finances in the event of an accident. Home insurance protects homeowners from financial loss in the event of fire, flood, or other disaster. And there's life insurance to protect people's assets in the unfortunate event of an untimely death. But annuities exist to account for a "problem" opposite unexpected death: They are designed to guarantee income even when people live longer than expected.

If you buy an annuity (that makes you an annuitant by the way), you are paying an insurance company for the rights to a contractual guarantee which ensures the insurance company will pay you income over a certain period of time to begin at a future date.

You may have heard finance people talk about "annuitization" and wondered what it meant. It's a fancy word for the process of turning on a traditional annuity's income stream. Once a contract is annuitized, there's no going back. At that point, regular income will be paid over the course of an annuity holder's lifetime. But here's the catch: If a policy holder dies the day after annuitizing, all the money he or she paid to the insurance company with the expectation of lifetime income may be forfeited. Often the insurance company is under no obligation to return those funds to an annuitant's inheritors. As you can imagine, that sets a pall over the annuity's many tempting benefits. We hear "annuitization" less and less these days, though. It's gone the

---

[21] Julia Kagan. Investopedia. May 17, 2019. "Annuity."
https://www.investopedia.com/terms/a/annuity.asp#axzz2B228dCaJ

way of the pager—this is just simply no longer the way the annuity business operates.

A Recent Twist

In the late 1990s, annuities got a makeover. People were tired of signing over a huge lump sum of cash without the guaranteed prospect of return. Annuitization essentially required annuitants to sign over the rights of inheritance to the life insurance company. Any money that remained in an annuity at the time of death was bequeathed to the managing annuity issuer. Children and other beneficiaries got squat. Does that sound like a lousy deal? It was, and retirees had had enough of it.

The new breed of annuity dispenses with traditional annuitization. Instead, many of today's annuities allow purchasers to exercise their annuities' income options and still leave the remainder to inheritors of their choice. Sometimes what's left even comes with appreciation.

Since insurance companies revamped the annuity concept, annuity sales have skyrocketed. According to one life insurance research organization, "in 2016, total fixed annuity sales hit a record-breaking $117.4 billion, 14 percent higher than" previous levels.[22]

While annuities have improved in the last few years, there is much variance in annuity types and in the benefits they offer. There are four basic annuity options. The following is not a thorough discussion of each category, but it should give you an idea of what each one does and the needs they are designed to serve. The four annuity types are immediate, variable, fixed, and fixed index.

---

[22] LIMRA. ThinkAdvisor. February 21, 2017. "Fixed annuity sales hit record $117.4 billion in 2016." https://www.thinkadvisor.com/2017/02/21/fixed-annuity-sales-hit-record-117-4-billion-in-20/

Immediate Annuities

Immediate annuities are the "traditional" standard that has existed for decades. They're not terribly popular these days for the reasons I explained earlier: After paying a lump sum, you immediately (hence the name) annuitize your contract and start receiving income. After annuitization, you cannot access the money you contributed nor can you or any heirs get it back unless you die within a period specified in the contract, a period-certain payout that specifies how much the contract will pay out by a certain date. When you die, the contract's remaining value is transferred to the managing insurance company.

Other annuity types focus much less on the need to annuitize. Instead, the annuity contracts are "deferred." You may fund your contract with a lump sum or over some period of time, and that money is left to accumulate interest. When you eventually begin drawing income, it does not come with the strict forfeiture feature of an immediate annuity.

Variable Annuities

Alright, let me get this one out of the way. I'll be frank—I don't believe in offering my clients variable annuities. In my opinion, they come with too much risk, excessive fees, and underwhelming benefits. Nonetheless, they remain a popular investment option, so I think it's important to understand how they work.

At its core, a variable annuity is an indirect stock market investment. Like all annuities, they're sold by insurance companies, but only through an agent licensed to sell investment products. As part of a variable annuity contract, the annuitant authorizes the insurance company to invest his or her money in the market by pooling the premiums of many annuity holders and investing in underlying sub-accounts (which typically invest in mutual funds). This feature is unique among annuities. A variable annuity thus doesn't provide one of the primary objectives in buying an annuity: Lower risk. Of all annuity types, variable is the only one that subjects your money to potential loss without protection, unless you pay additional annual costs for a guaranteed rider.

Now, there's a reason why variable annuities still sell: Higher risk means they hold out the prospect of higher return if market conditions are in your favor. But, in my opinion, it's not worth it, especially for those in or approaching retirement. The risk to reward ratio is too high for retirees and variable annuities come with other downsides on top of it. Variable annuities have numerous underlying expenses and management fees. When it's finally time to collect income, the insurance company will determine what you get based on the contract's value (unless you're purchased an additional guarantee rider, as I mentioned previously).

Potential for market loss and some of the higher fees make variable annuities a less than desirable retirement option for many.

Fixed Annuities

Fixed annuities represent the next evolution in annuity types. A traditional fixed annuity is pretty simple. The annuity contract comes with a guaranteed interest rate and when you're ready to start withdrawing from your investment, the insurance company will provide regular income for the duration of your life. In some cases, if you choose, a fixed annuity may continue to pay income to your husband or wife even if you precede your spouse in death. Fixed annuities also dispense with the obligatory forfeiture of principal that came with old-fashioned annuitization.

The downside to fixed annuities is limited potential for growth on your initial money. For many, however, the positives are enough to make fixed annuities a valuable retirement strategy. Guaranteed income for the entirety of your life is nothing to scoff at. And knowing exactly how much you can expect to receive provides a level of comfort. While a variable annuity is subject to stock market whims, a fixed annuity promises financial consistency.

Fixed Index Annuities

So far, we've discussed (1) immediate annuities, (2) variable annuities which introduce the potential for growth on investment but come with risk, and (3) fixed annuities which provide income guarantees but have limited potential for growth. Annuity number four is the fixed index annuity (FIA).

Fixed index annuities often have higher growth potential than a regular fixed annuity but without market participation or risk. In fact, most FIAs expressly protect against market downturns.

Fixed index annuities are not invested in the market, rather they have the opportunity to earn interest each year based on positive changes to an external market index, such as the S&P 500, subject to limitations commonly referred to as a cap, spread, or participation rate. For example, your contract may stipulate that credited interest may not exceed seven percent. If the S&P 500 gains three percent as of your contract anniversary, your FIA likewise increases three percent. If the S&P 500 skyrockets and records 40 percent growth, your FIA will only increase by 7 percent as per the cap in your contract.

But what happens if the stock market tanks? You'll notice that earlier I said FIAs follow stock market *ups*. I didn't say anything about stock market *downs*. Herein lies the beauty of fixed index annuities. If the market nosedives, you won't see any increase in your contract's value, but neither will you experience any loss. No matter how poorly the stock market performs, your FIA will never lose value due to market loss (although you could lose value due to surrender charges if you take excessive withdrawals).

Let's illustrate that in real figures. Let's assume you have $100,000 that you allocate to a fixed index annuity. In the first year, you receive five percent interest. That means, your end of year total is $105,000. In the second year, the stock market dips 10 percent. Does that make your end of year two balance, (a) $94,500 or (b) $105,000? Many of my clients, after the first time we discuss FIAs assume (a) is the correct answer. In fact, it is (b). Fixed index annuities do more than protect just your principal. They additionally guarantee you will never lose the interest accrued in years of positive index growth because of market loss.

What Does It Mean for You?

Let's be clear, annuities are not for everyone. And they're not an all-inclusive retirement plan. But, for some, annuities can make a fine, stabilizing addition to their investment portfolio.

It's important to make sure your plan has plenty of liquidity. Annuities, on their own, have a limited ability to achieve that goal. Insurance companies expect you to let your money sit over the course of many years while you work toward retirement. There's a time commitment involved when you purchase an annuity. The insurance company wants to know they will have your money and be able to use it for a period of time. To discourage early withdrawal, most companies impose surrender penalties for withdrawals in the early years. At most, you can expect to withdraw 10 percent of your value each year before retirement without penalty. Withdrawals will also be subject to ordinary income taxes, and a 10 percent tax penalty if you are under age fifty-nine-and-one-half. It's important that you do not put money into annuities that you will need soon because of their lack of liquidity.

That said, annuities offer greater protection than can be said of many other investment options. Instead of using a traditional annuity to provide pension-like income, it could be used to simply withdraw from as needed in the overall plan.

If you choose to use an annuity in your larger investment portfolio, , be sure to consult with your financial advisor first. You must be careful about jumping into an annuity contract lest it come with additional fees and/or unacceptable limitations or terms of withdrawal.

Chapter Six Key Lessons

• Think carefully before you withdraw income from an unstable source. That could cause unfavorable sequence of returns risk.

• Annuities can be used many ways. That can be good and not so good. Some annuities can be a stable source to draw income from.

401(k)s and IRAs

I f there's one thing I've tried to emphasize in this book, it's that retiring in the twenty-first century will probably not work with your parent's retirement strategy. There was a time when most of the working population stayed with a company for the duration of their careers. Loyalty was rewarded with consistent pay raises, added benefits and vacation time, sometimes even a gold watch! But none of that was the grand reward. No, the prize at the end of the road was a pension. The pension of yesteryear was a promise from your company to support you in your retired years as repayment for the decades of hard work you contributed to its success.

But the era of pensioned retirement was not all sunshine and roses. The security of pensions was only as strong as the companies backing them. What would happen to your pension if your former employer went out of business? In Chapter Three, we saw the answer to that question with the story of Studebaker. The once untouchable titan of automobile manufacturing was brought to its knees in the late 1950s, finally declaring bankruptcy in 1963. It was the first time that a major corporation failed to pay millions of dollars in "guaranteed" pensions to its retired employees.

The United Automobile Workers (UAW) labor union was mortified. Thousands of employees, many of whom had spent four decades on the Studebaker assembly line, had been robbed of their well-deserved pensions. The UAW set about lobbying for a revision to the pension system. Specifically, the organization demanded federal backing, a government supported pension insurance.

In response to UAW demands, one pension expert told Walter Reuther, the civil and labor rights activist who'd built the UAW into a formidable labor union, that the introduction of federal insurance would "reconfigure the 'incentives' of both labor and management." In other words, if the government got involved, the entire pension system would have to change. As things would turn out, that comment proved almost prophetic.[23]

In 1974, Congress passed the Employee Retirement Income Security Act (ERISA). Finally, federal legislation was in place to protect retirees and their assets. ERISA established the Pension Benefit Guaranty Corporation (PBGC) which insured private pensions. ERISA also added to the Internal Revenue Code (IRC), tacked on in 1978. The addendum was section 401, subsection k, to be exact.

ERISA was designed to hold companies accountable for the pensions they promised. It was supposed to ensure that pension plans were funded in advance so that in the event of bankruptcy, pension funds would be safe. But many companies took issue with having to set aside funds that could otherwise be used to expand business. From the moment ERISA was passed, employers looked for ways to replace their pension obligations. When someone finally discovered IRC section 401(k), the entire pension system was turned on its head.

Internal Revenue Code section 401(k) reads, in part, as follows:

"(k) Cash or deferred arrangements.

> *(1) General rule. A profit-sharing or stock bonus plan, a pre-ERISA money purchase plan, or a rural cooperative plan shall not be considered as not satisfying the requirements of*

---

[23] Roger Lowenstein. The New York Times. October 30, 2005. "The End of Pensions." https://www.nytimes.com/2005/10/30/magazine/the-end-of-pensions.html

subsection (a) merely because the plan includes a qualified cash or deferred arrangement.

(2) Qualified cash or deferred arrangement. A qualified cash or deferred arrangement is any arrangement which is part of a profit-sharing or stock bonus plan, a pre-ERISA money purchase plan, or a rural cooperative plan which meets the requirements of subsection (a)—

> *(A) under which a covered employee may elect to have the employer make payments as contributions to a trust under the plan on behalf of the employee, or to the employee directly in cash;"*[24]

Section 401(k) goes on for several more pages, but the important part, cryptic as it may be, is within the first few sentences. In simpler terms, section 401(k) permits employees to defer some of their compensation to retirement accounts managed by their employers. It took employers a few years to recognize the opportunity IRC section 401(k) afforded them: A 401(k) gives employers tax advantages for sponsoring employee retirement plans even if *employees contribute most of the plan's funding.*

As employers caught on to the unique benefits of 401(k) plans, pension plans quickly faded into obscurity. Why would a company obligate itself to pay for employee retirement when employees could pay for it themselves?

401(k)s and their corresponding individual retirement accounts (IRAs) are conduits that provide tax benefits by means of other assets. Typically, 401(k)s and IRAs are funded with mutual funds, stocks and bonds, and money market accounts. In the last few years, other options have become available. Some companies even include annuity options as part of their 401(k) plans.

The difference between traditional pensions and 401(k)s can be summarized in a one-word shift. While pensions were defined-*benefit*

---

[24] Bradford Tax Institute. "Internal Revenue Code Section 401(k)."
https://www.bradfordtaxinstitute.com/Endnotes/IRC_Section_401k.pdf

plans, 401(k)s are defined-*contribution* plans. Pensions outlined exactly what retirees could expect to receive. The onus was on employers to figure out how much it would cost to guarantee those benefits. The now-popular 401(k)s are more or less the opposite. Employers outline how much money they will contribute to your retirement (if anything at all), but what a retiree does with that money and how far that money will go in sustaining post-work life is left to happenstance. That one-word alteration has had a dramatic effect on the evolution of today's work and retirement landscape.

A Changing Landscape

The 401(k) shift marked a change in employer loyalty. Companies these days offer little in the way of guaranteed benefits to their workers. Many employees have followed suit and kept their loyalties to themselves.

A 2014 survey found modern U.S. workers stay with their employers an average of five years before moving on to better prospects. The fifty-five to sixty-four demographic in the survey showed a little more constancy, but most were still likely to leave their companies after about ten years.[25]

The trend shows no sign of slowing down. Millennials are three times more likely to change jobs than previous generations and 91 percent are unlikely to stay with their current employer for more than three years. According to a Workforce survey, 80 percent say their propensity to change jobs is because the notion of "loyalty in the workplace has changed."[26]

---

[25] Catalyst. May 23, 2018. "Turnover and Retention: Quick Take." https://www.catalyst.org/research/turnover-and-retention/

[26] Deb McCusker and Ilene Wolfman. Questia. 2019. "Loyalty in the Eyes of Employers and Employees." https://www.questia.com/magazine/1P3-36080751/loyalty-in-the-eyes-of-employers-and-employees

Peter K. Murdock, vice president of recruitment for Blackmon Mooring/BMS CAT, says the new definition of loyalty "pertains to the job at hand." Employees will work hard to learn specific tasks until they can perform them masterfully at which point, they will use their new talent to market themselves to new employers offering higher wages and better circumstances. "The mentality," says Murdock, "is, 'you pay me to do X, I do X, and we are even.' Whether the next step comes from within their current organization or they have to make a move, they have fulfilled their obligation and were loyal in doing so."[27]

That leaves a strange dichotomy in the secular world—neither employer nor employee is terribly concerned with the other's well-being. Work has become "transactional," says Murdock. Workers view themselves as the drivers of their own careers. It's too risky to trust employers with one's future. The traditional corporate ladder leaves employees powerless to the whims of their superiors. Today's employees have had enough. They're breaking the cycle.

This "take care of yourself" attitude is permeating the American workforce. If that sounds critical, let me be clear: That attitude is necessary to have a solid chance of achieving your goals in today's secular climate. What some employers would call selfish is in fact a reactionary change in perspective among workers to protect themselves from an employment field that often appears to care little about its labor force. These days, there isn't much in the way of reward for "sticking it out" with a company. Sad to say, employees are often not considered an investment. Instead, many companies view their workers as dispensable assets. That leaves us to care for our own well-being and the security of ourretirements.

---

[27] Peter K. Murdock. Forbes. December 28, 2017. "The New Reality of Employee Loyalty."
https://www.forbes.com/sites/forbeshumanresourcescouncil/2017/12/28/the-new-reality-of-employee-loyalty/#322be65b4cf3

The Three-Legged Stool of Retirement

When I first entered the world of financial planning, I heard many older finance guys preach the three-legged stool of retirement. The stool represented an ideal retirement with each leg symbolizing an essential retirement income source. The first leg was a company pension. Second was Social Security. Finally, third, and the least emphasized back in the day, was personal savings. The three-legged stool of retirement was a lovely analogy—only with each of the three legs could you sit firm and secure in your retirement prospects. How quaint.

But what happens when you cut off one of the legs? I don't know about you, but I imagine that sitting in a two-legged stool requires more effort and coordination than your average person is comfortable with.

The same is true of retirement planning. Most people these days will be dealing with only two of the original three legs: Social Security and personal savings. For many people, the bulk of their savings is housed in a 401(k). It may seem overwhelming to enter retirement with only Social Security and your savings, but it is possible. However, the importance of an integrated plan cannot be understated. Pensions afforded retirees the leeway to neglect retirement planning because someone else took care of it. These days the responsibility to ensure retirement success rests squarely on our own shoulders.

Making the Most of Your 401(k)

If you're one of the many soon-to-be retirees with most of your retirement savings housed in a 401(k) (or its nonprofit and government counterparts, 403(b) and 457), you'll want to ensure that you make the most of your plan.

Many employers incentivize contribution to their 401(k) plans with promises to match some percentage of your funding. Take advantage of it! Get as much as you possibly can from your employer. You've heard it said that nothing in life comes free, but the company match to your retirement contribution is about as close to free money as anything gets. If it's within your means, make the minimum regular contribution to your 401(k) to qualify for your company's match, whatever it may be.

During your working years, it's easy for your 401(k) plan to fade into the recesses of your mind. You probably set up a system of regular withdrawals from your paycheck to be added to your 401(k) before taxes. You may have selected the financial products in which your 401(k) is invested. But after those initial decisions, there isn't much to worry about.

However, when you decide to retire or move jobs, there are several important decisions that can impact the value of your 401(k) plan. At the time you terminate your employment, there are generally four options for your 401(k):

1. Leave the money where it is

2. Withdraw the money as cash at which point, you'll have to pay income taxes and sometimes a 10 percent extra federal tax if you are younger than fifty-nine-and-one-half (we'll come back to that).

3. Transfer the money to a different 401(k)

4. Roll the money into a self-directed IRA

There are pros and cons to each of these options. Your decision will depend on individual circumstances and it's best to consult with a financial professional to ensure that you make the best decision for your retirement longevity. Some 401(k)s are heavily dependent on the companies that offer them. It may not always be possible to transfer funds from one 401(k) plan to another. Or it may not be possible to leave the money where it is if your former employer carries a direct cash-out or rollover policy. The best course of action may thus require some creative thinking.

A Word on Taxation

When people tout the advantages of 401(k)s and IRAs, they often mention their tax benefits. It is convenient that with many 401(k) and IRA plans you can invest money and allow it to grow for many years without tax. Such plans are called tax-deferred or tax-qualified. Do not, however, confuse tax-deferred with tax free. Whether an account is labeled tax-deferred, tax-qualified, tax-preferred, or anything else, it only indicates the *time* when you must inevitably pay taxes. Whether it's up front or years down the line, you better believe that Uncle Sam will eventually come for his slice of the pie.

Whether your plan requires you to pay taxes from the get-go or defers taxation until after retirement does not serve as an indicator of quality. All other things equal, it doesn't matter much at what point you pay taxes on your retirement accounts. But your individual circumstances may make a tax-deferred account more or less appealing.

Many working people assume they will cut back in their retired years. As such, there's a good chance they will fall into a lower tax bracket. If that scenario fits your plans, a tax-deferred account may be the way to go. If you expect to have less income during retirement than in your working years, it makes sense to push back taxes as long as that's your choice.

I find that many soon-to-be retirees "plan" to cut back in retirement because they see no alternative. If they had their druthers, they wouldn't sacrifice their standard of living nor simplify after retirement. On the contrary, if money was no object, many retirees tell me they would capitalize on their extra time to do things they never could as a working person. If that describes your dream retirement, don't be so quick to discount the possibility of earning the same or even more income after retirement. With an integrated retirement income plan, you may be surprised to learn how far your retirement savings can go. Don't assume you'll be in a lower tax bracket after retirement unless that's genuinely where you'd like to be. For people who would benefit from a retirement account with taxes paid up front, a Roth IRA may be an advisable alternative to traditional accounts. We'll come back to that shortly. First, let's examine some of the limitations imposed on your IRA or 401(k) by the IRS.

Limitations

1. Contribution Limits. If you are contributing to a 401(k), 403(b), or 457 plan, you may not contribute more than $19,000 per year as of 2019. That figure varies slightly year-to-year according to cost of living adjustments. If you are over fifty, you are allowed to contribute up to $6,000 more per year. IRAs are more limited. With an IRA, the annual contribution maximum is $6,000 with an extra $1,000 allowed for contributors over fifty.[28]

2. Withdrawal Limitations. 401(k)s and IRAs are obviously designed to produce retirement income. As such, the IRS is not quick to allow withdrawals before retirement age which the IRS defines as fifty-nine-and-one-half. That's not to say that you *can't* access your money earlier, but it will come with stiff penalties. Normally these include early withdrawal fees, payment of income tax, and an additional 10 percent federal tax penalty. There are some exceptions to the rule. The most common are outlined in the following table.

---

[28] Internal Revenue Service. June 18, 2019. "401(k) Plans - Deferrals and matching when compensation exceeds the annual limit." https://www.irs.gov/retirement-plans/401k-plans-deferrals-and-matching-when-compensation-exceeds-the-annual-limit

Exception to 59 ½ Rule	Applies to IRA or 401(k)
Death of Account Holder	Both
Total, Permanent Disability of Account Holder	Both
First-time Homebuyer (up to $10,000)	IRA
Higher Education Expenses	IRA
Unreimbursed Medical Expenses (limited)	IRA
Separation from Employer After Age 55	401(k)

If the listed exceptions don't apply to your situation, it's safe to assume you'll be penalized for early withdrawal from a 401(k) or IRA. It's not uncommon for younger investors to realize after making an early withdrawal from their retirement account that 10 percent has been lost in penalties on top of income tax. Except under the most extreme circumstances, a 20 percent hit is not worth it. Since 401(k)s and IRAs should not be considered liquid assets before a certain age, it's safe to say that they are not the best option to serve as an emergency fund. Especially with younger people, I see many investors who have all their savings housed in workplace retirement plans. They may have plenty of money shored away in the event of an emergency, but they sometimes fail to account for the extra loss they'll sustain from early withdrawal fees and higher than expected taxes.

Required Minimum Distributions

Let's say you opt for a tax-deferred retirement account and choose to sit on that money even after having retired. At some point, you must pay taxes on the money earned. That's when required minimum distributions (RMDs) come into the picture. At age seventy-and-one-half, the US government requires you to withdraw something from your account. How much you're forced to withdraw depends on the size of your account(s) and your estimated lifespan.

RMDs are not to be trifled with. The government will get its share one way or another. If you neglect to withdraw RMDs and to pay income tax on them, you'll be slapped with a fine for *50 percent* of what the RMDs should have been. It's much better to withdraw on time and avoid the pain of sacrificing a huge chunk of your hard-earned savings.

Roth

As a final note, I'd be remiss to neglect Roth IRAs in a discussion of retirement accounts. Roth IRAs bear the name of Delaware Senator William Roth, who first proposed the idea. The Roth option to IRAs and 401(k)s was part of the Taxpayer Relief Act of 1997. The Roth version of an IRA or 401(k) is the same as its original counterparts in every way but one: You pay your taxes up front. When you eventually retire, withdrawals from Roth accounts are truly tax-free (assuming you are fifty-nine-and-one-half and the account has been open for at least five years). Since you don't have outstanding income tax to pay, Roth IRAs and Roth 401(k)s eliminate the government's need to impose RMDs.

Roth accounts may be a good choice if you can afford the taxes now and if you can reasonably expect that your taxes will be lower *now* than in later years. In the next chapter, we'll examine taxes in greater detail, but I'll give you a preview of what's to come: There's a good chance that your taxes right now are lower than they'll ever be again. That might make Roth IRAs an excellent addition to many retirees' investment portfolios for those looking for tax efficiency.

For people with traditional IRAs and 401(k)s, is there any way to convert to a Roth account? Yes, but there's a caveat. The IRS will permit you to transfer funds from a traditional account to a Roth, but you must pay the income tax due on the conversion. To the IRS, converting an account is the same as withdrawing the funds and putting them elsewhere. If you choose to withdraw $400,000 from a traditional account to fund a Roth, you may find yourself paying $100,000 or more in taxes. Is it worth it? That will depend on your personal circumstances. But suffice it to say, do not go about converting your account to a Roth without thoroughly considering the details.

Save, Save, and Save Some More

In today's retirement climate, more responsibility falls to the individual retiree to ensure the success of his or her post-work life than ever before. Personal savings is no longer the gravy on top – it's the main course. For many, a 401(k) or IRA is the primary retirement savings vehicle. How you intend to withdraw that money is an important part of a holistic retirement plan. It's especially important to account for the taxes owed on your retirement accounts. The next chapter will investigate that subject further.

Chapter Seven Key Lessons:

• This is not your grandpa's retirement (wait, is that something we have heard before?).

• A 401(k) is *not* an equal replacement for a pension

• Most of your retirement accounts (IRA's, etc.) are not pensions. Great care must be taken to get the most use out of them in your plan.

• One goal of the Money Master Retirement Plan is to identify tax optimization and penalty avoidance of these types of accounts.

Chapter Eight
Taxes

O h boy . . . Taxes. Where to begin?

In my experience, taxes may be the most overlooked facet of retirement planning. Taxes are an indelible part of life. No matter how much or how little we earn, the government will always look for its cut.

As good citizens we don't mind taxation. After all, it's only by means of our tax dollars that many essential government functions are funded. We need roads, bridges, schools, a military—everything that keeps society running and American citizens safe.

Most people would agree that taxation in the United States is fair. After all, demands for reasonable government taxation were among the first points of argument to instigate the American revolution in the 1760s. Tax law has evolved in the centuries since the founding fathers won our independence, and it has contributed to the growth of the world's leading country. Still, you'd probably agree, while we're willing to pay our fair share of taxes, no one wants to pay a cent more!

Many years ago, I heard a joke about taxes. It goes something like this: "What's the difference between tax evasion and tax avoidance?"

"About ten to fifteen years."

A real knee slapper, right? The joke is a bit corny, but it underscores an important point. Tax *evasion* is a federal offense. Tax *avoidance*, however, is the perfectly legal practice of ensuring that we do not pay more in taxes than the government expects.

But you may be thinking, "I've used an accountant for years for exactly this reason: So that I don't pay more taxes than I need to." That may be true, but a tax *professional* is not a tax *planner*.

I'm not talking about someone who examines a year's worth of receipts, forms, and papers, whom you see a few times between January and April, and who sends off your tax return in your behalf. In fact, those steps are only a small part of the bigger picture. Tax planning extends beyond your April filing. It's with a view to years of future taxes. Tax planning is about plotting every financial move designed to help keep the most money in your own pocket. For retirees, tax planning is especially important. When regular income is flowing, we may stand to overpay a bit come tax-time. But, when it's our responsibility to generate income for several decades of retirement, every dollar counts.

One often overlooked area of tax impact is the order of account withdrawal during retirement. According to Bill Reichenstein Ph. D, CFA, and Professor Emeritus of Investing at Baylor University, the order in which you withdraw your savings in retirement makes a significant impact on its longevity and value. These findings were published in an article entitled, "tax efficient withdrawal strategies." Frankly, it's a long and boring study. But it makes an important point: A sound retirement plan *must* incorporate consideration of withdrawal order. It's for that reason that our Money Master Retirement Plan includes tax planning as one of its major tenets.

Now, let me be clear, I am not a CPA. But as part of the team-based approach at my firm, we work with several tax experts to ensure that taxes are considered as part of the larger retirement planning process. Every penny that's saved in taxes is a penny we can put to work developing more retirement income. That's what it's all about for myself and my team.

Almost every new family my team has ever worked with has been poised to pay more taxes in retirement than necessary. Most just don't know any better. Many don't realize that with a few adjustments in the structure and formatting of their retirement portfolio they stand to save as much as thousands of dollars in annual taxes. After sitting down with one new family, we calculated that he could save about $300,000 over the course of his lifetime! What could you do with an extra $300,000 or even more?

I can't say for sure that you'll necessarily save that much money, but you can probably adjust your investment portfolio to keep some extra money away from Uncle Sam. These days especially, unique circumstances exist in the tax world that can have a profound effect on your retirement income.

A Unique Set of Circumstances

In the United States, tax law is something of a fickle proposition. It seems like every few years, the Internal Revenue Service comes out with a new and enlarged edition of its already overwhelming tax code. The most recent incarnation of the monstrous reference book is 74,608 pages long. For some perspective, that's longer than Leo Tolstoy's *War and Peace*, J.K. Rowling's entire Harry Potter series, and the King James Bible *combined*. And the tax code isn't just longer than the amalgam of those other books. Altogether, *War and Peace*, Harry Potter, and the Bible barely exceed half the IRS tax code's length. I bet you didn't realize there was so much to be said about taxes, huh?

The IRS itself admits the tax code is ridiculous. When the code was first published in 1913, it was only 400 pages long – a formidable tome, but manageable for the diligent reader. Since then, things have gotten wildly (can taxes get wild?) out of hand. In 2008, the Taxpayer Advocate Service's Annual Report to Congress from the IRS stated, "the most serious problem facing taxpayers is the complexity of the

Internal Revenue Code." That's a tactful way of saying the tax code is indecipherable for the average person. Despite its honesty, the IRS failed to address the problem it identified. Six years later it added another 14,564 pages to the tax code. I guess taxpayers understanding the tax code isn't high on the list of IRS priorities.[29]

To simplify things, I'm going to make a bold statement: Taxes may be lower *right now* than we'll ever see again in our lifetimes. Now, I can't absolutely guarantee the accuracy of that claim, but let me explain.

On January 1, 2018, President Donald Trump's tax reform plan went into effect. It's the single biggest change in tax law we've seen for more than thirty years, and it may be a gamechanger for people in and approaching retirement. Tax brackets and tax rates have been adjusted to our benefit. On top of that, the standard deduction for each bracket has substantially increased.

In the last chapter I talked about tax deferred retirement accounts. I'll address them again later in this chapter, but the most important takeaway is that tax-deferred does not mean tax-free. Money in a tax-deferred account will at some point be taxed. It can be now or later, but invariably the fed will get its cut.

For many years, financial advisors have preached deferment under the assumption that retirees will fall into lower tax brackets after leaving the workforce. That may be true of some retirees, but it doesn't necessarily translate to lower taxes. Taxes could increase again in 2026. That means taxes to be paid on tax-deferred accounts could be higher in the future.

It takes an in-depth examination of personal circumstances to decide how best to plan for taxes. Current tax brackets will not impact

---

[29] Jason Russell. The Washington Examiner. April 15, 2016. "Look at How Many Pages are in the Federal Tax Code", https://www.washingtonexaminer.com/look-at-how-many-pages-are-in-the-federal-tax-code

everyone in the same way. But one thing is certain: you should plan for taxes *now* to ensure you don't miss out on immense potential savings.[30]

Tax Brackets Effective 2018

Single Filers	Married Filing Jointly	Tax Rate
$0 – $9,525	$0 – $19,050	10%
$9,526 – $38,700	$19,051 – $77,400	12%
$38,701 – $82,500	$77,401 – $165,000	22%
$82,501 – $157,500	$165,001 – $315,000	24%
$157,501 – $200,000	$315,001 – $400,000	32%
$200,001 – $500,000	$400,001 – $600,000	35%
$500,001+	$600,001+	37%

TAX YEAR 2017 STANDARD DEDUCTIONS

Single Filers	Married Filing Jointly
$6,350	$12,700

TAX YEAR 2018 (TRUMP PLAN) STANDARD DEDUCTIONS

Single Filers	Married Filing Jointly
$12,000	$24,000

---

[30] Amelia Josephson. SmartAsset. January 23, 2019. "Here's How the Trump Tax Plan Could Affect You." https://smartasset.com/taxes/heres-how-the-trump-tax-plan-could-affect-you

The Good Times May Not Last Forever

Besides the Trump Tax Law, there's a second reason why taxes could go up in coming years.

Do you remember in Chapter Three when I talked about our national debt? As of this book's writing, the national debt sits near $22,000,000,000,000. That's $22 *trillion* with a big fat T. If you spent more than $50 million every single day for the next 1,100 years you still wouldn't reach $22 trillion. Anything in the trillions is confounding. It's more money than the individual person can fathom.

Where do you suppose the federal government will look to earn the money it needs to start paying off its tremendous pile of debt? You guessed it: Taxes. If the federal government wanted to wipe out the national debt strictly with taxpayer money, it would take almost $200,000 from each citizen.

My intention is not to scare you. The government will never demand so much from each American, nor is national debt a problem that the United States government plans to resolve overnight. But it's reasonable to suggest that taxes will increase in the future to address the mounting debt problem. All the more reason to capitalize on favorable circumstances while we have them.

So how can you use the information we've discussed to lower your retirement taxes?

Know Where You Stand

Before making any tax avoidance maneuvers, you have to know what tax bracket you fall in based on income minus pre-tax or untaxed assets. After carefully evaluating your taxable income, determine how close you are to the next lower or higher tax bracket. Ideally, you will reorganize income funds to fall into a lower tax bracket. But at a minimum, you must be careful not to inadvertently push yourself into a higher tax bracket. This is especially important when planning to gift large sums of money and with Roth IRA rollovers.

I had a couple come into my office a few years ago whom we'll call Charles and Cindy Schultz. Charles and Cindy were very accomplished, and they had built several large accounts from which to draw retirement income. Charles was sixty and a few months from retiring. With so many options, their biggest concern was which accounts should they withdraw from first when they stop working?

Charles had a large pension that had not been claimed yet. Cindy—who was sixty-two—was considering taking her Social Security benefit. A couple of factors made their situation unique. Charles had an account comprising only four stocks worth $420,000. He had paid $200,000 of after-tax money for the shares. This meant that they could expect to pay capital gains on $220,000, the gain from the sale of the stocks.

Charles was eager to stop working. When we first established his retirement plan, we made note that he might have a limited time opportunity to take advantage of when he stopped working. You see, he and Cindy made the decision not to claim his pension, nor Cindy's Social Security benefit. That allowed them to minimize the taxes owed on their $220,000 of built-in capital gains. In fact, having not claimed their pension and benefits, the Schultzes fell into a low enough tax bracket that they could live from that $220,000 for the first few years of retirement completely tax free. Their regular income was less than $50,000, and by selling just enough shares to recognize $30,000 in gains each year, they were able to stay beneath the $80,000 threshold for paying capital gains taxes (2020 rates). Then, later in retirement, they would spend the next $200,000 on which taxes had already been paid.

This strategy, called capital gains harvesting, would have multiple benefits. First, Cindy's Social Security benefit would keep growing by 6.5 percent per year for a few more years. Second, Charles' pension was able to defer longer, to age sixty-five, increasing his benefit. Lastly, the couple harvested the growth on their stocks tax free.

Current tax law in the United States allows for a married couple filing jointly to avoid capital gains tax if they make less than $80,000 in total taxable income (2020 rates). If Charles and Cindy would have had other income, they would still have benefited from this strategy, but their income wouldn't have been completely tax free. Of course, they had done all of this planning under the supervision of a CPA.

This situation was unique to Charles and Cindy, but it's not as uncommon as you might think. Several other ideas like this exist and I believe that most people are not taking advantage of them.

For example, it is common to see investors with a 60/40 (60 percent equities, 40 percent bonds) portfolio breakdown. Even if they have, say, three different accounts, all three would be set up as 60/40. You're probably familiar with this investment strategy; you may use it yourself.

But what if your financial advisor took one extra step and organized your investments according to the tax status of each account? Remember, Roth IRAs, taxable accounts, and 401(k)s are all treated differently. So, for instance, what if of your three accounts, the Roth was designated for growth, the 401(k)s (or traditional IRAs) were to hold mostly bonds, and the taxable accounts had lower turnover more tax efficient holdings? This could be done in such a way that your household portfolio still breaks down to a 60/40 ratio, but your overall tax situation would have improved. Roth grows tax deferred *and* does not force you to pull money out when you are age seventy-and-one-half like in Traditional IRAs and 401(k)s. Since the IRA or 401(k) requires you to pull money out to pay taxes, it's often best to allocate such accounts as less risky, lower growth, portions of your household portfolio.

Don't Assume A Lower Tax Bracket

If you can organize your finances to fall into a lower tax bracket, great! But don't assume that post-retirement you will automatically drop into a lower bracket. I know, after you quit working you won't be contributing to retirement funds anymore. You won't have work expenses. Transportation costs may decrease. Surely, you'll fall into a lower tax bracket, right? Not always. In fact, that kind of thinking has put many a retiree in a pickle.

Think of it this way: after retiring, do you really plan on sacrificing your lifestyle and standard of living? Almost everyone would say, no. So, will a few changes in expenditure be enough to lower your tax bracket? Maybe, maybe not. But in my experience, it often takes a more concerted effort to rearrange financial affairs to change your tax status.

I've found that many people spend more money in the first several years of retirement than they did when they still worked. They go out to dinner more often, they vacation more regularly, they invest in hobbies that they didn't have time for as working people. Eventually that lifestyle tapers off as age sets in, but rarely do expenses decrease. Rather, vacation money is redirected to cover health and long-term care. That's all fine for people who planned accordingly. It's the optimists who expected low (or even sometimes no) taxes in retirement that often find themselves struggling when the tax bills look more or less the same as they did in the past. Don't make the mistake of assuming a lower tax bracket.

A Word on 401(k)s and IRAs

We discussed 401(k)s and IRAs in the previous chapter, but they're important enough to warrant a brief recapitulation.

Almost everyone reading this book will have a 401(k), IRA, or an equivalent. Most variants of retirement accounts are tax deferred. In other words, we sock away money for years without paying tax on it.

But the taxman cometh.

When you reach age seventy-and-one-half and have not already started drawing from your 401(k) or IRA, you will be forced to draw some money as per required minimum distributions (RMDs). Those withdrawals will fall under taxable income. If you neglect to take your RMDs, the IRS will impose a penalty of 50 percent of any RMD money you ought to have withdrawn, and that's on top of your ordinary income taxes. Even if you make no other plans for your 401(k)s and IRAs, please, *please* do not neglect to take RMDs when necessary.

Of course, if you've elected for a Roth 401(k) or Roth IRA, you will not be required to withdraw at any age. That's because your taxes have already been paid. In light of today's tax environment, a Roth account is worth serious consideration. Unless you stand to fall into a tax bracket with much lower percentages, it may be worth capitalizing on the current low tax rate. Many have saved by converting their traditional retirement account funds to a Roth account while they are in a lower tax bracket or while their tax bracket has a lower taxable percentage. However, I don't advise making that conversion without the watchful eye of a financial professional. Poor execution of tax strategy can at the very least fail to save you money. At worst, you may end up overtaxed with less in retirement savings than you expected.

Planning for the Long Haul

Taxes aren't a fun subject. Most people avoid the topic until tax season rolls around when they're forced to file a return. Grueling as it may seem, a proactive approach to tax planning can make a big difference in the funds available for your retirement goals. We often think of taxes from year to year, but we ought to consider a long-term strategy with a view to saving money over several coming decades.

We often hear stories of the world's wealthiest people saving incredible sums of money in taxes. Sometimes, underhanded business practices are involved. But, more often than not, it's just that many wealthy people know how to use tax rules to their advantage. They're skilled at organizing money so only the minimum is taxed.

You can employ the same strategies. It may take some effort, but with the help of a financial professional, the process can be relatively painless. You may not stand to save as much as the world's richest people, but any savings is money that can work toward creating a better retirement.

Chapter Eight Key Lessons

- Understand and potentially organize retirement savings by tax account types (taxable, tax deferred, tax exempt).
- Consider Roth contributions or Roth conversions.
- If you estimate your future tax bracket you might be able to prepare to better navigate the lowest possible tax bracket.
- Consider consulting a financial and tax advisor to help you find the right withdrawal order of your accounts to optimize tax efficiency.

Chapter Nine

Don't Let Emotion
Get the Better of You

"We're expecting stocks to shoot up,
but we just don't know which ones and when."

Bear Stearns was days from financial collapse. Its Chief Executive Officer, Jimmy Cayne, was nowhere to be found.

Bear Stearns was a titan of the investing world. Although it was the smallest investment bank on Wall Street, Bear Stearns had survived countless financial setbacks and

107

economic downturns. It was there before the Great Depression, and had dutifully pulled through. It survived the infamous, "Black Monday" in 1987, the worst stock market crash in Wall Street's history. It had withstood the tech bubble crash of the early 2000s. Now, Bear Stearns was staring down another crisis: The housing bubble of 2008.

In July 2007, a pair of Bear Stearns hedge funds collapsed. The firm had made a risky bet on mortgages and it didn't pan out. At the time, Jimmy Cayne was in Nashville, Tennessee, playing in an exclusive bridge tournament that forbade cellphones. Even upon his return, however, Cayne was unaffected by his company's pending demise. Despite looming disaster, Cayne maintained his lavish and carefree lifestyle, often taking long weekends to play golf and bridge at locations around the country. If he wasn't out of town, Cayne still couldn't be bothered to address the company's issues. According to Alan "Ace" Greenberg, Bear Stearns CEO from 1978 to 1993, rather than work, Jimmy Cayne "preferred to be home in his pajamas playing bridge on his computer."

By March 13, 2008, the crisis was reaching a head. Bear Stearns executives convened in a last-ditch effort to pull together emergency funding and save the faltering investment firm. Guess who wasn't present for the meeting?

That's right, Jimmy Cayne.

He was in Detroit at a professional tournament of his favorite pastime: Bridge. You can look it up yourself. Cayne apparently placed fourth. Meanwhile, Bear Stearns was drowning.

Just three days later, the company was bankrupt and out of options. On March 16, 2008, the company's leaders agreed to a government-backed fire sale. Bear Stearns was acquired by JPMorgan Chase for a measly $2 a share. The total sum they paid amounted to less than the value of the firm's office building. It was the first company to go under as part of what would become the greatest financial crisis since the Great Depression.

Bear Stearns, the Wall Street monolith, was no longer.

According to the writers at *Time Magazine*, Jimmy Cayne was squarely to blame. In fact, he was among a handful of important Wall Street figures whom the magazine blamed for the entire 2008 market crisis and ensuing Great Recession. Think about that for a second. While "plenty of CEOs screwed up on Wall Street," the article reports, "none seemed more asleep at the switch than Bear Stearns' Cayne. He left the office by helicopter for three-and-a-half-day golf weekends. He was regularly out of town at bridge tournaments and reportedly smoked pot. (Cayne denies the marijuana allegations.) Back at the office, Cayne's charges bet the firm on risky home loans . . . But that was only the beginning. Bear held nearly $40 billion in mortgage bonds that were essentially worthless."[31]

Looking back now, more than ten years after the fact, the fall of Bear Stearns is still shocking. It was probably avoidable. But Jimmy Cayne drove his company into the ground. His problem can be summarized in a single phrase:

Failure to recognize risk.

That probably sounds familiar. I talked about the dangers of misgauging risk all the way back in Chapter Two. But the idea bears (no pun intended) review. Jimmy Cayne underestimated the dangers that threatened his company and it cost him everything. When Bear Stearns was absorbed, Cayne reportedly lost $1 billion in his own money.

"I didn't stop it," Cayne later said, "I didn't rein in the leverage." Indeed, Cayne *could* have stopped it. He wasn't incompetent. In fact, the story of his ascent to CEO of a major Wall Street investment bank encapsulates the American dream. From humble beginnings as a scrap metal worker and taxicab driver, Cayne had risen by merit of his intelligence and business savvy. When he inherited chief management

---

[31] Time. "25 People to Blame for the Financial Crisis."
http://content.time.com/time/specials/packages/article/0,28804,1877351_1877350_1877327,00.html

of Bear Stearns in 1993, the company's stock value was only $16. By 2007, at the height of his career and the company's success, stock value was $173 per share.[32]

So, what happened? What went wrong?

Success bore overconfidence; overconfidence bred disaster.

The Dangers of Emotional Investing

What's the investor's number one adversary? It's not complicated investment vehicles, it's not hidden fees, and it's not taxes. It's not even market volatility.

The investor's worst enemy is *emotion*.

Emotional investing is the very reason why financial advisors exist—because individual investors too easily succumb to emotion and tend to make poor decisions with their money. Often, the most dangerous emotion is overconfidence. If overconfidence can lead an accomplished CEO of an investment bank to make decisions that ultimately tank his company, you'd be wise to consider whether it can harm your investment strategy as well.

At its very core, investing combines the application of several basic rules. For example, everyone knows the adage, "buy low, sell high." In practice, however, emotion can make even a simple rule difficult to follow. It combines overconfidence in one's own financial prowess with fear of loss when things don't go as planned. To illustrate this fact, imagine a hypothetical investor name Helen.

Helen is your average investor. Investing is not her profession, but she knows that it's important to invest her money to develop a retirement nest egg. For many years, Helen has taken a half-hearted

---

[32] Matt Egan. CNN. March 16, 2018. "The stunning downfall of Bear Stearns and its bridge-playing CEO." https://www.cnn.com/2018/09/30/investing/bear-stearns-2008-crisis-jimmy-cayne/index.html

approach to investing. But she's getting older now, and she figures it's about time that she seriously considers her plans for the future.

One day, Helen gets a tip from James (her office friend who works in the cubicle adjacent to hers) about a stock that's been performing well. "All the TV finance guys are raving about it," James explains enthusiastically. "It's a surefire way to rake in some easy money."

Helen is ecstatic. This is exactly the sort of thing she's been looking for to boost her investment portfolio. Excited as she is, however, Helen is no fool. She's too smart to throw money at an investment opportunity solely on the recommendation of her coworker, friendly as he may be. So, Helen decides to wait a while to watch the stock's movement and verify whether or not it's really gaining value. Over the course of a few weeks, Helen is pleased to see the stock's value trending upward. She decides that it's finally time to buy in.

Every morning, Helen checks her stock's value when the market opens. She's pleased to find that its price has continued to climb in the few weeks since she decided to join the action. She starts to fancy herself something of an investing prodigy. She really hit the jackpot with this investment. She's getting richer by the day. At this rate, she may be able to retire within a few years. Maybe she'll make investing her full-time occupation and travel the world on the interest she makes from her well diversified and robust portfolio.

Now, everyone knows the stock market is cyclical. Helen knows that too. But it doesn't prevent her from feeling just a bit disappointed when one morning she wakes up to find that her stock has decreased in value. It's not the end of the world; she's still sitting on a much higher share price than was she originally paid. But Helen can't help but feel a twinge of apprehension. But she's read about this before; it's not wise to sell out just because there's a bad day. The prudent thing to do, she reasons, would be to wait and see what happens over time.

Unfortunately for Helen, her stock's value continues to fall. In fact, it's plummeting. Still, she clings to the hope that one of these days she'll wake up to find her stock has skyrocketed to new all-time highs.

Alas, it doesn't seem meant to be. The stock is only going down. The TV finance people are no longer praising its merits. James has been uncharacteristically mute at work. The whole world seems to be closing in around her and Helen wants out. Eventually, she awakens to find that her stock has fallen beneath the price at which she purchased it. And thus, snaps the camel's back. Helen drops her stock like a hot potato.

A few weeks later, Helen's curiosity gets the better of her. "How is that stock faring these days?" she wonders. After work, Helen logs into her online stock trading software and looks up the devilish stock that had caused her so much grief. "I hope the whole company tanked," she thinks to herself. But then...

Oh no! The market has gone back up!

That wily old stock is again on the rise but now it's too late for Helen to make back the money she lost. She bites her lip, struggling to contain her anger. How could this be? That stock looked like it was headed for zero, for goodness sake! She never expected it to turn around this quickly. Now what is she to do? She could buy in again and hope for a different outcome. Or maybe it's best to invest her money elsewhere. In fact, maybe she'll just throw in the investing towel altogether and bank on her 401(k) to provide her with future retirement income.

Helen's story is exaggerated in part, but it's not unrealistic. Many a would-be investor has ridden the same emotional rollercoaster. In fact, it's well documented that Helen's behavior is typical of individual investors. Experts call it the "cycle of investor emotion," and it normally ends with a demoralized investor and richer Wall Street executives.

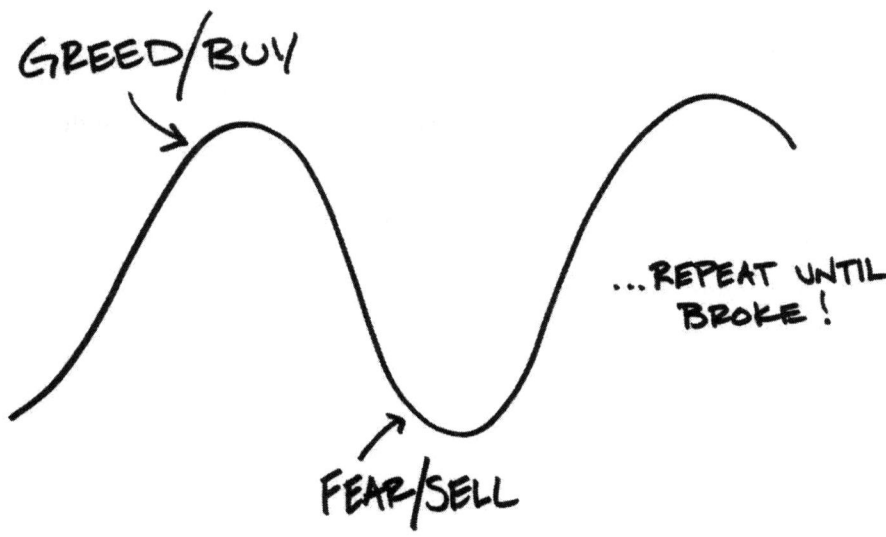

GREED/BUY

...REPEAT UNTIL BROKE!

FEAR/SELL

BEHAVIOR | GAP

There are at least two key problems in Helen's approach to investing. First, Helen was ill-equipped to thoroughly evaluate her investment of choice and she got in over her head. She didn't have the resources or information to accurately evaluate the investment vehicle she chose. She didn't know what to expect after investing her money, nor how to respond when things didn't go her way.

Second, Helen lacked accountability. There was no one to provide objective feedback and advice when her situation got sticky. Without accountability, emotion runs rampant.

To combat these two problems, we use a software program that monitors accounts. It is a system designed to help combat typical investor behavior error. Software can keep investors from hitting the panic button. Every day, it monitors your account values to ensure that your objectives are maintained. If the account reaches a predetermined point at which action is required, it sends you a text message and it sends a message to your advisor. Systems like this can make retirement planning less stressful, but it still requires a qualified advisory team with the background and knowledge to use it correctly, to analyze its output and give sound advice to help you choose the investments that best suit your needs. And after having invested your money, an advisor is there to make sure that you continue to make responsible decisions even when emotion would have you cash out and run for the hills. A financial advisor is an objective third party—an intermediary between you and your investments—that operates devoid of emotional involvement.

Sorting Through the "Noise"

FACTORS THAT <u>DRIVE</u> RETURNS

1- BEHAVIOR
2- % IN STOCKS
3- % IN SMALL STOCKS
4- % IN VALUE STOCKS

*MARKET TIMING, STOCK PICKING, CNBC, YOUR BROTHER-IN-LAW...

BEHAVIOR GAP

A study from 2011, published in the *Journal of Wealth Management*, explored "the behavior of individuals involved in financial decision making." The researchers were primarily interested in finding whether individual investors from the general populous could effectively 'self-regulate' their investing decisions or if the average investor would stand to benefit from an investment advisor's oversight. The study concluded, "all of the predictions of the theory are borne out by the data. In short, an important service provided by investment advisors . . . is the barrier the advisor provides to prevent the individual from aggressively trading and thereby losing money." In other words, a financial advisor can help you to make better investment decisions and to earn more money. Who wouldn't want that?[33]

A good financial advisor serves as the "voice of reason" helping you to sort through the "noise" of the investment world. A financial advisor helps you to avoid the distractions of fad investments and overhyped trends. Do you remember Aesop's fable about the tortoise and the hare? The moral of the story: Slow and steady wins the race. That is especially true when it comes to investing. And yet, something as basic as *waiting* is often the most difficult pill for an investor to swallow. A DALBAR study found that "investors lack the patience and long-term vision to stay invested in any one fund for much more than four years. Jumping into and out of investments every few years is not a prudent strategy because investors are simply unable to correctly time when to make such moves." Unfortunately, jumping from investment to investment is just one of several mistakes that investors commonly make. [34]

A big part of what we do as a financial advisory team is coach people to make wise decisions. There's no room for emotion in money management, and yet, ironically, there are few subjects that elicit a

---

[33] Maymin, Philip and Fisher, Gregg S., Preventing Emotional Investing: An Added Value of an Investment Advisor (September 10, 2010). Journal of Wealth Management, Spring 2011, Forthcoming; NYU Poly Research Paper; https://doi.org/10.3905/jwm.2011.13.4.034. Available at SSRN: https://ssrn.com/abstract=1675187

[34] Lance Roberts. MarketWatch. October 21, 2017. "Opinion: Americans are still terrible at investing, annual study once again shows." https://www.marketwatch.com/story/americans-are-still-terrible-at-investing-annual-study-once-again-shows-2017-10-19

more emotional response than money. A good financial advisor will help you to remove emotion from the retirement planning process.

A Vanguard Advisor's study called "Advisor Alpha" set out to determine whether financial advisors really can add value to the retirement planning process through "relationship-oriented services such as wealth management and behavioral coaching." In other words, the study examined whether a financial advisor can really help you earn more money. Every dollar counts these days in a retirement climate that offers little forgiveness for error. If you're going to hire an advisor, you want to know that it will benefit you. After examining several metrics of advisor contributions like general guidance, suitable asset allocation, cost-effective implementation, and rebalancing, Vanguard concluded that a financial advisor adds at least "3 percent to your net returns." Moreover, the study emphasized that this was a minimum expectation. In some cases, professional assistance "may offer much more than 3 percentage points of increased returns."[35]

The stakes are higher for today's retirees than ever before. Baby boomers must contribute more to their own retirements than previous generations. That makes prudent investment all the more important.

Our job as a team is to help you answer your financial decisions now and in the future. When choosing an advisor, ask yourself, 'what experience do I want to have?' If the process an advisor offers matches your answer to that question, your retirement planning will be a much happier endeavor.

A stock is a stock and a bond is a bond—that never changes. Financial products and holdings are becoming a commodity. But the experience you have during the financial planning process, that can vary widely. I have observed that many people's experience in retirement goes something like this: they call up their advisor and ask if they can buy a new boat. The advisor says either, "yeah, we've had a

[35] Vanguard. 2019. "Quantifying Your Value to your Clients." https://advisors.vanguard.com/iwe/pdf/FASQAAAB.pdf

good year, go ahead," or, "no, sorry, we've had a bad year, you should probably scale back the spending."

That kind of advisor-client interaction works, but I'd say it isn't the most rewarding way to live in retirement. What if the experience could be different? What if planning was an exciting phase of life? In our practice, people call up and say, "I want to buy a boat—please see how we can add this to my financial plan and send me the update so that I can see if I want to buy it." These people have more control and they're much more in tune with their financial status and retirement prospects.

It's often overlooked that a key purpose of an advisory team is to keep you in proper perspective with your plan and with what's going on in the world. That has tremendous value. I've mentioned several times in this book that today's retiree is at a disadvantage compared to my grandpa's retirement era. However, with monitoring systems and a team of advisors working to provide solutions to twenty-first century challenges, it doesn't matter that it's not your grandpa's retirement—it can be a success nonetheless!

Chapter Nine Key Lessons:

- We're only human, and emotions and behavioral bias can cause unfavorable results.
- Systems, processes, and advisors can help us achieve better results.

Chapter Ten
The Financial Planning Process

I f you're not already retired, I'd encourage you to practice retirement before you get there. That probably sounds a bit strange, but I'll explain.

When my grandpa retired at sixty, he did it abruptly. He'd been working one day and next he was up at 5 a.m. with a fishing pole in one hand and a golf club in the other. It was something of a shock for grandma. She hadn't spent so much time with this man in almost forty years! Eventually the shock caught up to my grandpa too. After the initial fun wore off, he realized that he wasn't emotionally prepared for retired life. Work had been a critical facet of everyday life for several decades. Now he just didn't know what to do.

If I remember correctly, it took my grandfather about five years to settle into retired life. His career officially ended when he turned sixty. But until age sixty-five he did little jobs here and there—building fireplaces mostly. The money he made in those years helped supplement his income until Medicare kicked in, but it was primarily to keep him busy while he figured out what he wanted to do with the rest of his life.

Many people likewise have difficulty easing into retirement. To make the transition more comfortable, they may practice in the years leading up to it. They may find things like new positions within the same company. They may take a new job working part time. I worked with a lady once who'd had a very successful career as an executive at Texas Instruments. When I asked her what she wanted to do in retirement, she said, "Well, I think I'll start out as a lunch lady at the local junior high school!" Can you believe that? She embraced the lighter responsibility of that position and the joy of being around children.

What ideas do you have? Could you be a consultant to your previous company? Could you take a similar position that carries fewer responsibilities and lower stress? Or maybe you'd like to take up a trade or hobby that's completely different than anything you've ever done. Whatever you want to do, you should have thought about it long before you retire. Perhaps you could retire *to* something, not *from* something. People often think about getting away from work. Then six months after retirement they come into my office and say, "what do I do with myself?" Okay, so that's a little bit of an exaggeration. But it's true in essence. You don't want to find yourself wasting precious retired years because you just don't know what to do.

I have a homework assignment for you—the same one I give to all new families who visit my practice. Go write down a list of things you'd like to do that will make retired life meaningful. You may find it more challenging that you anticipated when you actually put pen to paper. I'll give you some ideas based on what people have told me in the past: Take a photography class, write short stories, do ancestry work, maintain a garden for your church, finish a new degree, take up hobbies like woodworking, quilting, or a new instrument—the options can go on and on.

When you choose to work with an advising team, make sure they're asking these types of questions too. Remember, this is your new phase of life. What do you want the experience to be like? You get to choose, but you'll need a financial plan that supports your goals.

Before anything else, make sure a financial advisor is prepared to optimize your Social Security and to stress test your portfolio.

To **Optimize Your Social Security**, it's best to use purpose-built software. A good Social Security analysis will produce a multi-page report that reveals various choices specific to your needs. It will highlight key considerations such as lifetime cumulative benefit differences between strategies, different survivor's benefits for the last living spouse, and pension offsets. This allows you to make informed decisions. Getting such a report is easy. Any advisor willing to discuss Social Security typically subscribes to a software designed to achieve the aforementioned results. Simply input your benefit amount and your age and the report should be ready in seconds.

It is also imperative to **Stress Test Your Portfolio**. This is sort of like an x-ray. A reporting agency called Morningstar (along with numerous others) can summarize your current group of portfolios. Most people have more than one account. Without a program like Morningstar, it would be difficult to evaluate your total household combined return, fees, standard deviation, and maximum drawdown. Knowing how far your current household portfolio has drawn down is critical when you're in the preservation or distribution phase of life. This report gives you the starting point information needed to create an income distribution plan.

The **Income Distribution Plan** is the first strategy of five that make up what my firm calls the Money Master Retirement Plan (MMP): A holistic approach to retirement planning. It helps ensure your expenses can be paid month to month for the rest of your life. It typically includes an income and expense analysis, Social Security optimization, inflation planning, and spousal-continuation planning.

Most people want an income distribution plan, but don't have one. The closest they have is an account statement or a product illustration. Instead, they should have something more substantial. For example, perhaps something like the image below. Mind you, income distribution plans are unique to each person, so your picture will look slightly different than this example.

Distribution Strategy

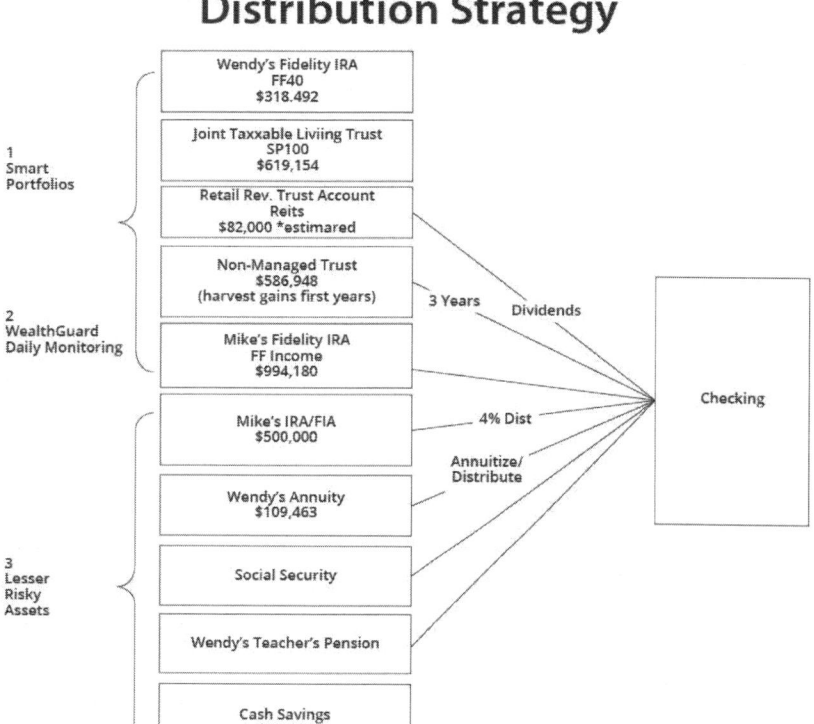

People need an easy-to-follow, step-by-step guide that has been created based on their unique situation. It should include who does what and when, dates like when should you take your first distribution, and which accounts will be used in what order. It should also account for the exact day you and your spouse will claim Social Security, the exact month when you should apply for Medicare, a reminder to take required minimum distributions, and any other remaining tasks to do.

Next in the MMP is a rules-based **Investment Plan,** driven by a formula, that uses smart risk re-balancing designed to help you protect your assets. It might include IRA and 401(k) planning, risk management planning, daily portfolio monitoring, and institutional money management, all performed by a team of professionals bound by fiduciary standards who puts your needs and goals first.

This is where the portfolio stress test from Morningstar becomes important. It lets us identify fees, risk, return, and anything that may be useful in improving your overall plan. Moreover, it allows us to point out simple systems that can be employed to monitor your accounts and help ensure your target values are always met.

Year after year, at any given moment people want to know: (a) how much money do I have? (b) how am I doing financially? and (c) what's being done to protect my hard-earned money? Portfolio monitoring services are essential in answering such questions.

A **Tax Optimization Plan** includes tax-optimization strategies, Roth conversion analysis, charitable giving, required minimum distribution plan analysis, and account withdrawal order analysis.

There are plenty of possible tax efficient ideas to be shared. Which are most relevant to you? For instance, you might be near retirement and still have twenty years left on your mortgage. Maybe you are aggressively paying down your mortgage but not saving any money in your 401(k). Perhaps it would be of greater long-term benefit not to pay down the mortgage and to save instead. Then again, saving in a 401(k) is not always advantageous; it may be wiser to direct funds into an after-tax account or Roth. It's hard to say in the moment what course of action will prove most successful over time. It can be difficult to make decisions when the benefits will not be evident for many years. But a tax optimization plan can model future wealth scenarios based on tax related decisions that you make now.

A **Health Care Plan** is designed to help you protect yourself against rising health care costs—budgeting for Medicare Part B & D, and analyzing options for a long-term care plan.

Just as with the tax examples above, health care decisions can be difficult to make when their effects are not readily apparent. How your resources are uniquely allocated will determine which long-term care options will serve you best. Not everyone can justify traditional long-term care insurance, but there are many other ways to address the extended care issue. This part of the Money Master Retirement Plan allows us to rule in or out the options that may apply to you.

Finally, a **Legacy Plan** is developed by working collaboratively with a qualified estate planning attorney. The goal is to help you to maximize your estate and income tax planning opportunities and to ensure assets are distributed to your beneficiaries with minimal probate costs.

Don't DIY; Get Help!

The world in which we live has become infatuated with the do-it-yourself (DIY) lifestyle. And I get it. In many respects, it's satisfying to do something yourself and it can often save you money. But there's a time and a place for the DIY attitude. I often say there are two areas in life where you should never do-it-yourself—your *health* and your *wealth*.

Most people wouldn't dispute the fact that it's unwise to handle medical situations on their own. And yet, we probably all know some people who loathe visits to the doctor. It's understandable, but when a serious medical condition arises, it would be folly to resist professional medical attention.

In the same way, we should not be flippant with our wealth. There's just too much on the line. In many ways, retirement is the culmination of your working years. It's the time during which you can finally relax and enjoy the fruits of your labor. But it requires careful planning and expertise to help you achieve your retirement dreams. You wouldn't perform surgery on yourself; why does it make any more sense to leave your retirement up to chance?

My goal in this book has been to outline important tenets of retirement planning. Still, I suggest that every reader consult with a retirement professional before making weighty financial decisions. This book has established several important guiding principles, but their application may require a professional touch. Everyone's circumstances are unique and require an individualized financial plan. Don't compare your situation to your neighbor's, coworker's, brother's, sister's, or anyone else's. To do so would be a mistake. To assume that someone else's financial plan will perfectly suit your needs is even worse.

Imagine visiting a department store to buy a new pair of shoes. You find a pair that catches your eye, but the display model is a size 7. You wear a size 11. You find a worker and ask if he can retrieve a size 11 from the back for you to try on. "Oh, I'm sorry," the worker says, "we don't have any 11s in the back. We only sell size 7."

That would be ridiculous!

It is likewise absurd to contend that one-size-fits-all financial plans will adequately prepare people of differing backgrounds and circumstances for the challenges of twenty-first century retirement. Take the time to find an advisor that fits the experience you want. You won't regret it. The assurance it can afford you cannot be measured just in the dollars and cents that you'll earn from a strategic investment portfolio. It can also add tremendously to your entire quality of living. Stress is a killer. You want to enjoy you retired years, but to do that, you must reduce stress and find new meaningful ways of relating to this new season of life.

Remember: Retirement stress can stem from unanswered questions, such as:

- Will I have enough money to last my entire life?
- If my spouse dies, how will my lifestyle change?
- How do I know I am making an optimal Social Security decision?
- Could I be more tax efficient?
- How much risk am I really exposed to?
- Am I doing anything different today than I was back during the last market correction?

You may have felt your blood pressure rise a bit just from reading those questions. I get it. Fortunately, it's possible to answer such difficult questions. In fact, that has been the purpose of this book. I hope you've learned a lot about retirement and financial planning. Understandably, there will be yet more for you to learn. I encourage you to find an advisory team that matches your goals and ideals. It can make an immeasurable difference in simplifying the retirement process and improving your retired years.

Retirement these days is harder than it used to be. When my grandfather retired, it was hard *not* to have what one needed to live comfortably. Between company pensions and Social Security, most people had everything they needed. Personal savings was the icing on the cake. The same cannot be said of today's retirement climate. Social Security is an unsure proposition, and pensions have all but gone the way of the dinosaur. Personal savings is now the foundation of retirement income, and many people do not feel prepared to fund their post-work lives. But it doesn't need to be that way. You can be confident that the retirement of your dreams is possible. It's true, it's not your grandpa's retirement. But with a good financial plan, and a trusted team at your back, your retirement can be every bit as successful!

Please, feel free to reach out to us with any further questions about your retirement. We would be happy to assist you:
www.brindleandbay.com   **214-988-9178**

About the Author

Through his financial planning firm, Brindle & Bay Wealth Management, Nicolas Davis helps families focus on creating integrated retirement income and wealth management strategies. He believes all money spends better with a written and tracked plan. He holds the CERTIFIED FINANCIAL PROFESSIONAL™ designation as well as the Chartered Financial Consultant and Retirement Income Certified Professional designations. Alongside his team of professionals, Nick takes a big-picture approach with families to assist them in pursuing their financial goals. He thoroughly informs his clients about the advantages and disadvantages of their financial decisions and helps them create and execute financial, tax and estate strategies that can guide them throughout retirement.

Nick is a member of an advisory board for an investment portfolio that was recognized as an Inc. 500 top 10 fastest-growing small business in 2016 and 2017. In that role, he provides insight on improving the financial advisory experience for retirees.

Nick's media show, *Money Master Podcast*™, can be heard via podcast. Nick has been published or quoted on CNN Money and Forbes.com and is a sought-after speaker on the topic of retirement income planning.

Nick lives in Texas with his wife, Connie, and four children.

Nick holds Texas insurance license No. 2314827.

Acknowledgments

I attempted to write a book several years ago and it never made it out of my office computer. After a hundred pages of writing I realized that I needed a team. Although it's true speaking aloud is effortless for me, the written word communicates much differently. I found the communication style to be an entirely different skillset.

There were times during this project when I became fearful I had been neglecting my team at Brindle & Bay. They wondered where my mind was on several occasions—with my blank stare off into the distance. I would consider myself a creative person, and fortunately but unfortunately, creative people are never satisfied with their work. They wonder, "Can I say it better? Is there another example? Will everyone know what I'm talking about?'"

Because of such perfectionism, this book almost didn't make it out of my office computer, either.

However, I love to read. I know the benefit of the written word, the sharing of ideas, and the personal benefits I've received from the knowledge that comes from books.

I am a very technical person, and that tends to get me into the weeds. My brain is stuck somewhere between an engineer and a public speaker. It sounds like a contradiction in personality, but that's me. I'm like an analyst who talks a lot. Despite this side of me, though, I did not want this to be a technical book. I wanted this because the purpose of this book is to communicate a message to more people than simply the engineers (you know who you are). You might scoff at the simplicity and surface level examples provided in the book, but I hope you enjoy the stories by understanding their purpose.

Crafting this book has taken me much time, determination, and patience on my part. Because of all this, I want to thank my family for allowing my absence on weekends and evenings. I've been fortunate enough to have a fantastic researcher, Lars Dolder. Lars is responsible for the copy editing and research behind some of the stories, and for pulling me back into simplicity many times.

Lastly, I want to acknowledge my grandma Betty for reminding me of the details of my grandpa Leroy's retirement. Grandpa Leroy led by example and I swear it seems like every day I wonder if he would believe that I am doing a good job with investing and financial planning. He did not face the issues that we face today, and so I wonder if he'd appreciate the solutions I use.

I'm not a creator of anything new or fancy in financial planning. I'm a good follower, researcher and implementer. And, for that, I am grateful for all the great advisors and technicians who have taught me good financial planning, including the team at Formula Folios, Jason Wenk, the American College of Financial Services, and the Certified Financial Planner curriculum. I'm grateful for the various conversations with the more experienced practices out there (gray-haired guys).

I appreciate and value the many dedicated conscientious financial advisors that I know. Anytime I find a competent financial planner, I cherish the relationship we build.